Spring flowering bulbs
1986

English translation by
Mr. J.M. Visser

with technical assistance from

Dr. A.A. De Hertogh
Department of Horticultural Science
North Carolina State University
Raleigh, NC 27695-7609

● *© Copyright and realization HORTICOLOR s.a.r.l., publisher. B.P. 69200 VENISSIEUX - France*
No ISBN: 2-904176-01-2/Dépôt légal: March 1985.

● *No part of this book may be reproduced in any form by print, photoprint, microfilm or any other means without written permission from the publisher.*

● *Reproductions NOVA PHOTO-GRAPHIK (Austria) - © Copyright*

● *The color photographs were for the most part produced by Johan GROOT (Holland)*

● *The editing, the research and the choice of photos was done by Robert CATTERINI (Sté Horticolor).*

● *Design and layout: Studio HORTICOLOR*

● *For their co-operation and advice we thank:*
– INTERNATIONAL FLOWER BULB CENTER in Hillegom (Holland)
– LABORATORY FOR FLOWER BULB RESEARCH in Lisse (Holland)
– JAN VAN DER HOEK of Van der Hoek's Experimental Forcing Association
– the photographers who kindly supplied the missing photographs.

● *Printed in Austria*

Spring-flowering bulbs

This book was prepared by a group of garden specialists who are in constant contact with the growers and suppliers of flower bulbs.

The primary goals of this book are: (1) to describe the best and most spectacular species and cultivars, (2) to assist the gardener in selecting bulbs for the desired areas and uses, and (3) to give cultural information to provide the possible results under the climatic conditions that exist in your area of North America.

Because the book has or will be published for many countries, all species are classified using their botanic (Latin) names. This is followed by the English (American) equivalents in the technical and descriptive texts, English names, if there are any, will be used. The index at the end of the book enables the reader to quickly find the species and cultivars that are described.

This book is not a botanical encyclopedia or treatise. Therefore, very rare species and cultivars are not described. Propagation techniques that are sometimes very difficult to carry out or are performed only by the bulb grower are not covered in depth. Also, only a few paragraphs are devoted to the very interesting history of the bulbs.

With a few exceptions, only the flowering spring bulbs are described in this book. This was done in order to avoid confusion between bulbs that must be purchased, planted in fall and then flower in spring or early summer with those bulbs that must be planted in spring and then flower in late summer or early fall. A second book will cover the spring planted bulbs.

Bulbs are among the first flowers of the new year and herald the coming of spring. There is a wide selection for gardens, balconies and indoor forcing. The major purpose of this book is to illustrate those species which have been specially cultivated for these purposes and will, with a little care, provide enjoyment each time they are used.

Characteristic Dutch Landscape in April-May.

Some historical facts about flower bulbs

The history of flower bulbs, even though it is very interesting, will not be described in detail. The first and primary goal of this book is to provide cultural information on bulbs for the gardener. Nevertheless, it is interesting to know that flower bulbs can be traced back to about 1800 B.C. The Madonna Lily (**Lilium candidum,** see page 74) decorated the frescos and pots of ancient Crete and as a species it has not been changed since that time.

The Pharoahs cultivated Anemones, Lilies, and **Narcissus.** The Greeks and Romans used these flowers along with Crocuses, Hyacinths and Gladioli for their religious and funeral ceremonies. It is only much later that we find the first reference to the most important commercial flower bulb, the Tulip. Its introduction into Europe dates back to 1554. It's attributed to a Flemish diplomat who was at the court of Sultan Soliman, The Magnificent. He dispatched tulip bulbs to Vienna and they were subsequently introduced into The Netherlands. Since then, the tulip has played a very important part in the Dutch economy. In

the 17th century, there was an enormous economic speculation in striped and "flamed" varieties and the so-called 'Tulpmania' resulted. From the originally introduced species, numerous hybrids have been bred and cultivated and these are now the most available cultivars of tulips.

Where are bulbs produced?

The Netherlands, also known as Holland, produces the majority of flower bulbs that are sold world-wide. It has the soils and climate, which are very stable and ideal for many bulbs. In addition, the Dutch have accumulated a great deal of knowledge on all aspects related to bulb production. There is, however, some spring-flowering bulb production in the U.S., Canada, Japan, France, and Great Britain.

Visiting Holland in April or May, when the fields are in full flower, is a real experience. The Hyacinths, Tulips and **Narcissus** offer spectacular and unforgettable views. Also, there are many miscellaneous bulbs in flower at various times during the flowering season. Those individuals who love flo-

wers, in general, and, specifically the spring-flowering bulbs, must visit the famous Keukenhof, a park consisting of 28 hectares (70 acres) where the majority of the cultivated species and cultivars are grown for exhibition purposes. Keukenhof is sponsored by the Dutch bulb growers and exporters. It first opened on March 22, 1950 and has been open each spring since that time. Almost a million visitors come to Keukenhof each year. It is a must for all gardeners.

What are bulbs?

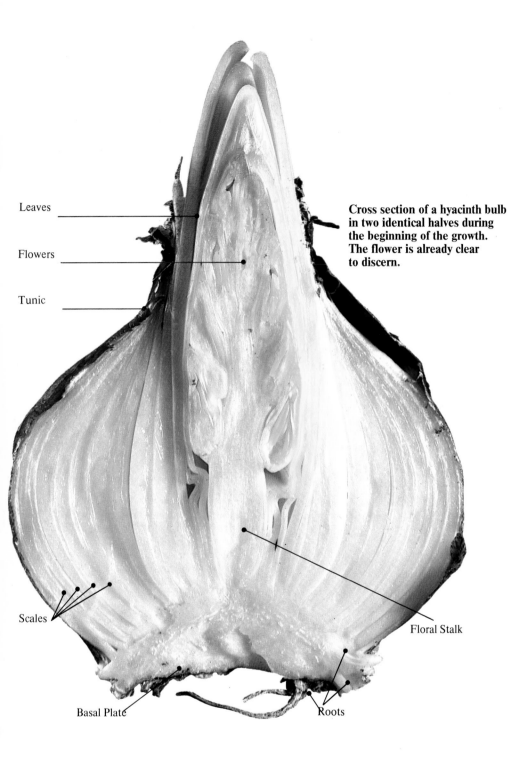

Leaves

Flowers

Tunic

Scales

Basal Plate

Roots

Floral Stalk

Cross section of a hyacinth bulb in two identical halves during the beginning of the growth. The flower is already clear to discern.

The general growth and development pattern for most fall planted bulbs is as follows. After the bulbs have been harvested in the summer and given proper post-harvest temperature treatments, they form the future flower(s), leaves and bulblets (See hyacinth example on left). Thus, they are ready to flower in the spring and also to have organs that will provide for another year's growth. In the soil or on water, for those species that can be forced on water, the roots develop. They take up the water and nutrients and also anchor the plant. As the bulbs root and then flower, they lose some of their storage reserves, but after flowering this loss can be replenished through photosynthesis. Some bulbs may, however, not accumulate sufficient food to enable the bulbs to grow as large as needed and consequently they will not flower as prolifically in the second season. For other species, it is necessary to remove the bulblets from the original bulbs and to give them special handling (see Chapter p. 152 on Propagation). The key to success with bulbs is to know which ones have perennial type reproductive systems, e.g. NARCISSUS and Hyacinths, and which ones have annual replacement systems, e.g. Tulips and Crocuses. This will be described under the individual bulb description sections. However, the majority of the bulbs, should be left in the ground and they will continue to flower year after year. The potential for perennialization will also be given in the individual bulb sections. Some examples of bulbs that readily perennialize are: CROCUS, LEUCOJUM, Lilies, MUSCARI, NARCISSUS, and Scillas.

The major true spring flowering bulbs are:
ALLIUM
AMARYLLIS (Hippeastrum)
CHIONODOXA
ERYTHRONIUM
FRITILLARIA
IRIS DANFORDIAE
IRIS HOLLANDICA (Dutch iris)
IRIS RETICULATA
HYACINTHS
LEUCOJUM (Snowflakes)
MUSCARI
NARCISSUS (Daffodils)
ORNITHOGALUM UMBELLATUM
OXALIS DEPPEI
PUSCHKINIA
SCILLAS
TULIPS

The term 'bulb' is given to those plant species that have underground, fleshy storage organs. The primary purpose of these organs is to permit the species to survive under adverse climatic conditions. Strictly speaking not all the species with underground storage organs can be called 'bulbs'. There are also corms, tubers, tuberous-roots, rhizomes, and enlarged hypocotyls. In some cases, it is easy to distinguish between the various storage organs, other times it is difficult to draw a definite line between one type and the other. Thus, in this book, they are, for convenience sake, called 'Bulbs'. After flowering, the bulbs store food in their underground organs. This enables them to grow again in the following year. Leaves and roots play important role in the process of food storage. They are responsible for providing the sugars, starch, proteins, nutrients and water that are needed for survival, and subsequent growth and development.

True bulbs

The true bulb consists of the following tissues (see hyacinth example above):
- a tunic, which is a skin that protects the fleshy bulb scales (some bulbs, e.g. Lilies, have no tunic).
- fleshy scales, which are the primary storage tissue.
- the shoot, which in many cases, consists of preformed flowers and leaves.
- the basal plate from which the roots grow and on which the scales and shoot(s) are attached.

The corms

Corms are composed of the following tissues:
- a tunic, which is skin that protects the scales.
- the basal plate, which contains the nutritive reserve.
- the buds that grow on the top of the corm.
- the roots that grow from the basal plate.

Corms often look like true bulbs. They are mostly round and they tend to be flattened. The key difference is that the basal plate tissue predominates and the amount of scale tissue has been greatly reduced. The roots grow from the basal base. The shoots develop on the top of the corm and the fleshy basal plate contains most of the storage reserves. All corms reproduce by annual replacement, i.e. new corms are developed from the old corms. Thus, photosynthesis from the leaves and nutrients and water taken up by the roots are very important to survival of corms.

The principal spring-flowering corms are:

CROCUSES
BRODIAEA (Triteleia)
IXIA
SPARAXIS

Crocus corm

The tubers

Tubers are different and readily are distinguished from bulbs and corms by the absence of the tunic. They are composed of enlarged stem tissue. It is often difficult to recognize the upper part of the tuber from which the eyes or buds grow, but they can be detected with careful observation. When tubers have been harvested, care must be taken not to damage the eyes. The shoots develop from them. Tubers can be either cylindrical and flattened or odd shaped. In contrast to bulbs and corms, they tend not to produce new tubers, but generally speaking, they enlarge during the period of vegetative growth.

Principal spring-flowering tubers:

ANEMONE
CYCLAMEN REPANDUM
ARUM CORNUTUM

Anemone tubers

The rhizomes

Rhizomes have no tunics. They are underground stems. They differ from tubers in shape, generally being long and oval. They have eyes and perennial roots. They do not produce new stem tubers, but become larger during the vegetation-period.

Principal spring-flowering rhizomes:

CONVALLARIA MAJALIS (Lily-of-the-Valley)

Convallaria Majalis-rhizomes

Healthy Tulip bulb

Diseased Tulip bulbs

The tuberous roots

In contrast to tubers and rhizomes, they are fleshy roots and can be either single or branched. Buds develop on the old stem-base, or crown as it is called. Tuberous roots grow during the vegetation period.

Principal spring-flowering tuberous roots:

EREMURUS
RANUNCULUS

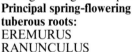

Ranunculus tuberous roots

6

Purchasing bulbs

Spring-flowering bulbs must be planted in the fall and quality bulbs are essential for successful flowering. Bulb growers and exporters give their bulbs not only special treatments to protect them against diseases and insects but also to insure proper flowering. Thus, when they are sold they are in a healthy condition. It is possible, however, that under improper post-harvest storage or transport conditions that the bulbs may become diseased or damaged. If bulbs show any signs of disease, i.e., they are too soft, they should not be purchased. In addition, as a general rule, do not wait to buy bulbs at the end of the marketing season. The longer they are kept in the retail stores, garden centers, etc., the poorer the quality becomes. This does not mean, however, that bulbs bought at the end of November and immediately planted will not flower, but there is a risk involved.

Bulbs are marketed in many ways. They are sold in bulk, in packages, and through mail order houses. It is essential that the consumer know the name of the species and cultivar. This aids in knowing where and how to plant the bulbs in garden. Bulbs come in various heights and colors and they have different flowering periods. Hints on planting are either written on the packages or special instructions are provided. Normally only top-sized bulbs are sold (See Table below). This insures that when the bulbs are given proper care they will flower. The actual size of the bulbs varies greatly not only between species but also from cultivar to cultivar.

Bulb size is important

Bulb size determines the vigor of the plants and the number and size of the flowers produced. Therefore, it is advisable to purchase only top-sized bulbs. Generally, the size given is the circumference measurement of the bulb. (See Amaryllis example below).

Market Sizes of Some of the Major Bulb Species.

Species	Size Range (Cm)		
	Top Sizes	Medium Sizes	Smallest Sizes
AMARYLLIS (Hippeastrum)	32/up	26/28	22/24
ANEMONE	8/up	6/7	5/6
CROCUS VERNUS	10/up	8/9	7/8
DUTCH IRIS	8/up	7/8	6/7
FRITILLARIA IMPERIALIS	20/up	18/20	–
HYACINTHS	19/up	16/17	14/15
MUSCARI	10/up	8/9	7/8
NARCISSUS (1)	DN I	DN II	DN III
RANUNCULUS	8/up	6/7	5/6
TULIPS (2)	12/up	11/12	10/11

(1) Narcissus are sold on the basis of size and the number of bulb noses.

(2) These sizes do not apply to most of the botanical tulips, since many of them never grow to this size and are sold as smaller bulbs.

size 12+   size 11/12   size 10/11

The above photograph shows the results of the diverse Tulip bulb sizes: Large bulbs produce larger and stronger flowers than the smaller bulbs.

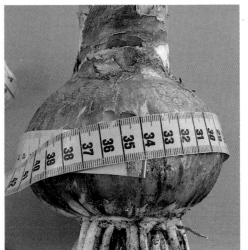

For example, tulips are sold as 10/11, 11/12, and 12/up cms. This means that the 11/12 bulbs have a minimum circumference of 11 cm and a maximum of 12 cm. The 12/up means that the circumference of the smallest bulb is 12 cm and that some of them may be as 13 or 14 cm in circumference. In contrast, daffodils (NARCISSUS) are sold as: DN I, DN II or DN III, the DN stands for Double Nose. The "I" indicates it is the largest double-nosed bulb, while the III is the smallest size of this category.

Thus, there are various sizes and shapes of bulbs that are marketed and the terminology can vary (see examples on pages 8-11). The sizes of some of the major spring-flowering bulbs is given in the adjacent Table.

This is how bulbs are measured: Here is the circumference of an Amaryllis bulb (cm).

Principle bulbs – how they look
(the pictures represent actual size)

ALLIUM SPHAEROCEPHALON

ALLIUM MOLY

ALLIUM AZUREUM

ALLIUM NEAPOLITANUM

ALLIUM ALBOPILOSUM

ALLIUM GIGANTEUM

ALLIUM AFLATUNENSE

AMARYLLIS

ANÉMONE BLANDA

ANÉMONE FULGENS

ARUM ITALICUM

BRODIAEA LAXA

CAMASSIA

CAMASSIA
CUSICKII

CHIONODOXA

ERANTHIS HYEMALIS

CROCUS VERNUS

CYCLAMEN COUM

EREMURUS

ERYTHRONIUM

FRITILLARIA MELEAGRIS

FRITILLARIA IMPERIALIS

GALANTHUS

FRITILLARIA PERSICA

GLADIOLUS
BYZANTINUS

HYACINTHUS MULTIFLORUS

HYACINTHUS

IRIS
RÉTICULATA

IRIS HISTRIOIDES
"MAJOR"

DUTCH IRIS

IRIS BUCHARICA

IRIS DANFORDIAE

IXIOLIRION PALLASII

LACHENALIA TRICOLOR

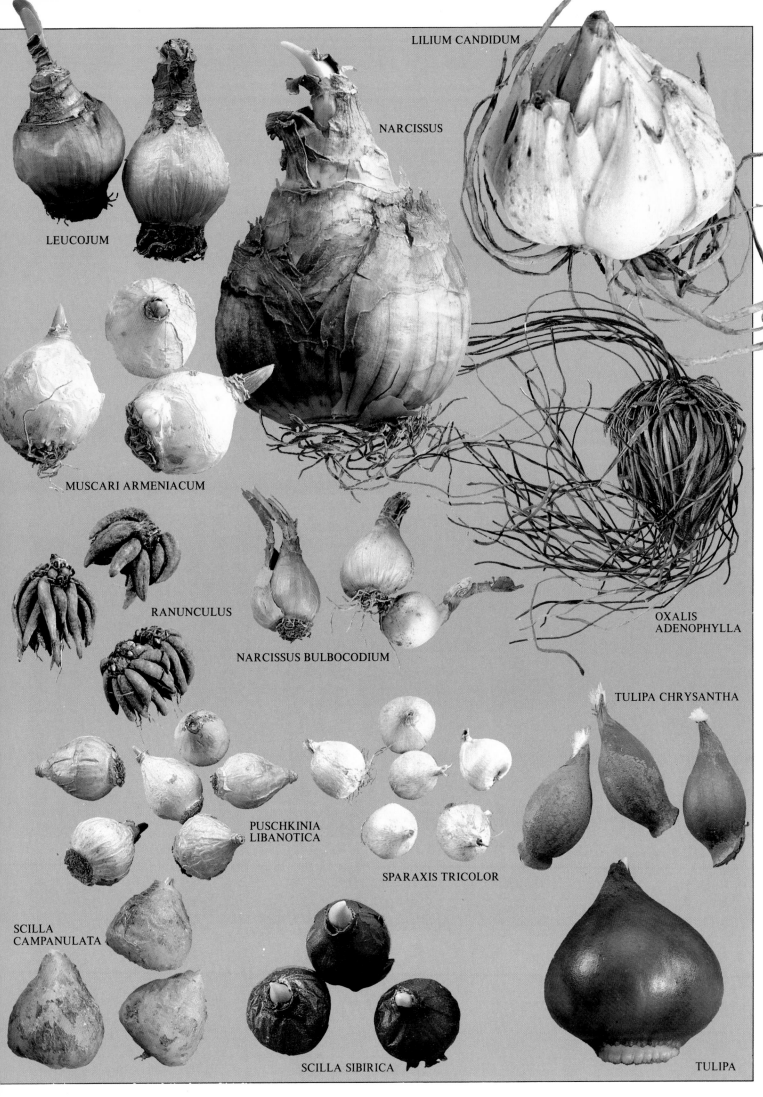

LILIUM CANDIDUM

NARCISSUS

LEUCOJUM

MUSCARI ARMENIACUM

RANUNCULUS

NARCISSUS BULBOCODIUM

OXALIS
ADENOPHYLLA

TULIPA CHRYSANTHA

PUSCHKINIA
LIBANOTICA

SPARAXIS TRICOLOR

SCILLA
CAMPANULATA

SCILLA SIBIRICA

TULIPA

11

General planting and growing instructions

The growing of spring-flowering bulbs in the garden is very easy. Even beginning gardeners can have spectacular results. The reason is that in most instances, at planting time, the bulb contains either the embryonic flower or the potential to develop the flower shortly after planting. To obtain the best results, however, one must pay attention to a few key requirements for the bulbs.

General instructions for all fall planted bulbs are given in this chapter. More detailed information on the individual species and cultivars is provided in the respective sections.

Basic growth and development requirements

Spring-flowering bulbs have an absolute annual requirement of alternating seasonal temperatures of: warm (summer) - cool (fall and winter) - warm (spring). This cycle is called 'Annual Thermoperiodism'. Thus, for those bulbs that are to be used outdoors, they must be planted in the fall, rooted and overwintered for at least 10-12 weeks and then they will flower in the spring. There is, however, a variation in the basic winter hardiness and cold requirements of the bulbs described in this book. For instance, tulips are generally very hardy and require 12 or more weeks of cold. In contrast, Dutch Iris are not very hardy and only require 6 weeks of cool (above freezing) temperatures. Thus, tulips tend to do best in the climatic zones 4 to 7, while Dutch Iris do best in zones 8 and 9. These individual bulb requirements will be given in the individual species descriptions.

This book also contains a chapter on Indoor Bulb Forcing for the winter months (see page 17). The bulbs used for this purpose include bulbs like tulips, hyacinths, and **Narcissus** that have an absolute cold requirement and also bulbs like **Amaryllis** and Paperwhite **Narcissus** that do not. That is why a special chapter has been devoted to this specialized use of flower bulbs.

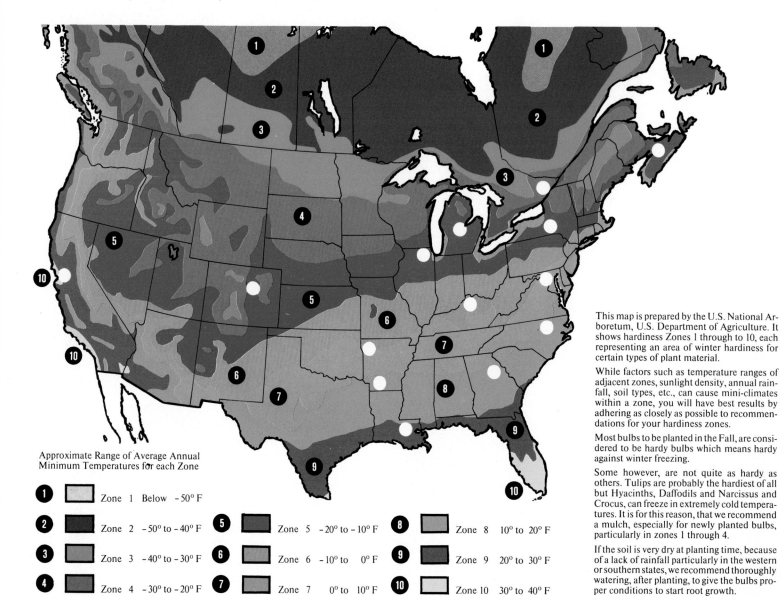

Approximate Range of Average Annual Minimum Temperatures for each Zone

1 Zone 1 Below – 50° F

2 Zone 2 – 50° to – 40° F

3 Zone 3 – 40° to – 30° F

4 Zone 4 – 30° to – 20° F

5 Zone 5 – 20° to – 10° F

6 Zone 6 – 10° to 0° F

7 Zone 7 0° to 10° F

8 Zone 8 10° to 20° F

9 Zone 9 20° to 30° F

10 Zone 10 30° to 40° F

This map is prepared by the U.S. National Arboretum, U.S. Department of Agriculture. It shows hardiness Zones 1 through to 10, each representing an area of winter hardiness for certain types of plant material.

While factors such as temperature ranges of adjacent zones, sunlight density, annual rainfall, soil types, etc., can cause mini-climates within a zone, you will have best results by adhering as closely as possible to recommendations for your hardiness zones.

Most bulbs to be planted in the Fall, are considered to be hardy bulbs which means hardy against winter freezing.

Some however, are not quite as hardy as others. Tulips are probably the hardiest of all but Hyacinths, Daffodils and Narcissus and Crocus, can freeze in extremely cold temperatures. It is for this reason, that we recommend a mulch, especially for newly planted bulbs, particularly in zones 1 through 4.

If the soil is very dry at planting time, because of a lack of rainfall particularly in the western or southern states, we recommend thoroughly watering, after planting, to give the bulbs proper conditions to start root growth.

The spring flowering season for fall planted bulbs

Because of the wide range of bulb species that are available, the spring flowering season for fall planted bulbs is approximately 4 months long. It starts with **Crocus** and **Eranthis** and ends with the Allium's and **Brodiaea laxa**. There is a range of heights from 2-3 inches (5-7.5 cm) to 2-4 feet (50-100 cm). Also, the color range is tremendous. There are solid reds, yellows, pinks, lavenders and a wide range of multi-colored flowers. Also, the shapes and sizes of the flowers range from 1 inch (2.5 cm) to 10 inches (25 cm). Thus, there are bulbs for everyone.

Purchasing and preplanting storage of the bulbs

When purchasing bulbs, the best criteria to follow is that they must be firm. Also, buy early to get the best selections and quality. In addition, as described earlier, purchase the proper bulb size to insure flowering. The size and/or number of flower(s) is directly related to the size of the bulb. It should be pointed out that small nicks or a loose skin (tunic) generally do not affect the development of the bulb. In fact, a loose tunic aids in inspecting for diseases and this condition also encourages rapid rooting after planting. After purchasing, keep the bulbs cool until they are planted. The storage temperature should be below 60°F (18°C), with 50-60°F being best for most fall planted bulbs. Be certain, however, to keep bulbs away from ripening fruit since they produce ethylene and this can cause flowering disorders, especially with tulips.

Bulb soils

Good drainage is absolutely essential for spring bulbs! If your soil is mostly clay, use one of three techniques to improve drainage. **First,** you can mix in an organic amendment such as peat-moss, compost, aged pine bark, etc. up to 50% in volume; **second,** use a sloped garden area; or **third,** the bulbs can be planted in raised flower beds. If your soil is mostly sand, add an organic amendment to increase water and nutrient holding capacity.

Soil pH is also critical! The pH of your planting area should be in the 6 to 7 range. If you need assistance in this area, contact your local county extension office.

Bulb sites

Bulbs can be used in formal beds, informal borders and perennial beds, ground covers, rock gardens, grass banks, lawns, shrubs and wooded areas. For perennialization, it is best to avoid planting them near heated basements.

FALL PLANTING GUIDE FOR SPRING FLOWERING BULBS

EASY PLANTING FOR BEAUTIFUL SPRING BLOOM

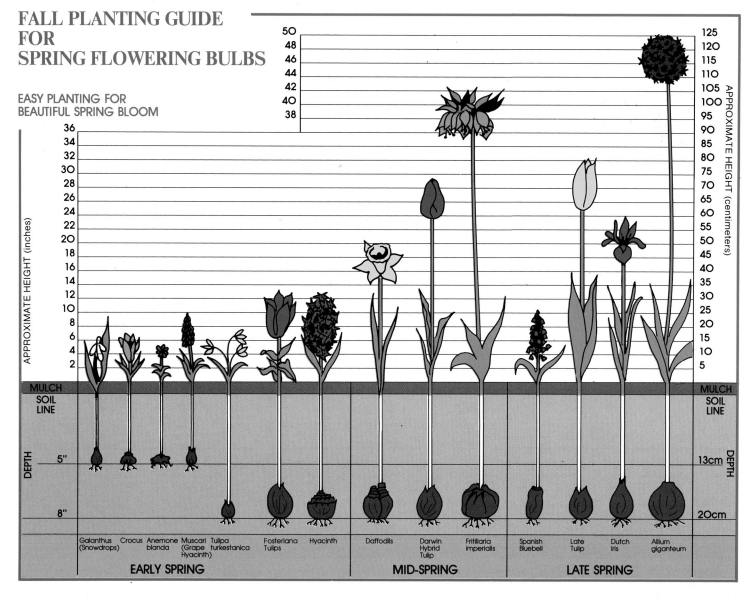

EARLY SPRING							MID-SPRING			LATE SPRING			
Galanthus (Snowdrops)	Crocus	Anemone blanda	Muscari (Grape Hyacinth)	Tulipa turkestanica	Fosteriana Tulips	Hyacinth	Daffodils	Darwin Hybrid Tulip	Fritillaria imperialis	Spanish Bluebell	Late Tulip	Dutch Iris	Allium giganteum

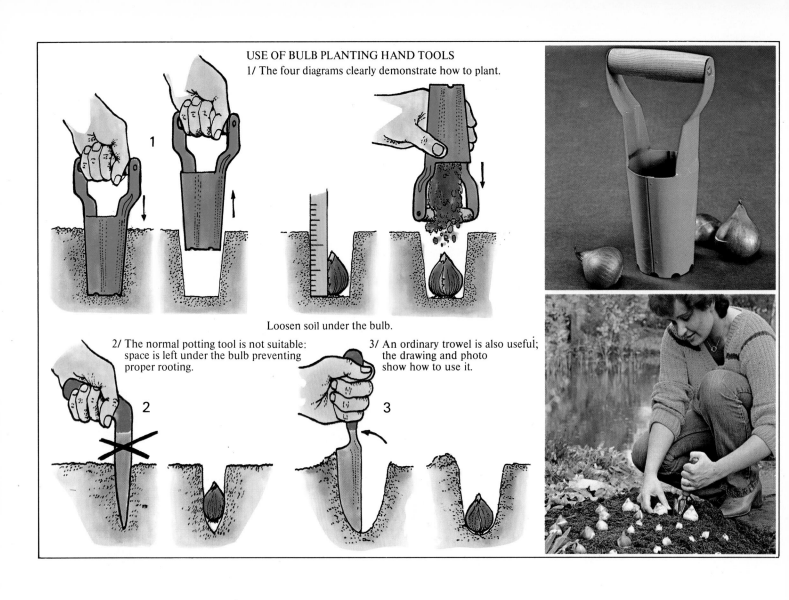

USE OF BULB PLANTING HAND TOOLS
1/ The four diagrams clearly demonstrate how to plant.

Loosen soil under the bulb.

2/ The normal potting tool is not suitable: space is left under the bulb preventing proper rooting.

3/ An ordinary trowel is also useful; the drawing and photo show how to use it.

Light

In general, spring-flowering bulbs do best in areas which do not receive direct sunlight during mid-day, especially during the hot summer months. This is particularly true for climatic zones 7 to 9. However, there are some bulbs that prefer full sun or shade and these requirements shall be mentioned in the respective bulb sections.

When to plant?

Spring and early summer flowering bulbs must be planted in the fall in order to develop a root system and to satisfy the cold requirement of the bulbs. It is best, however, to wait until soil temperatures are below 60°F (16°C) before planting. This means that gardeners in northern climatic areas will plant earlier (September or October) than those living in southern areas (November to early December).

How to plant?

First, excavate the area to be planted (See illustration on page 15 and above). The depths given in the planting chart (page 13) are measured from the base of the bulbs to soil level. Thus, small sized (1 inch (2.5 cm) in height) bulbs are planted 5 inches (12.5 cm) deep. Large sized (2 or more inches (7.5 cm) in height) bulbs are planted 8 inches (20 cm) deep. These depths of planting help to protect the bulbs agains frost, animals, and physical damage due to hoeing, etc. After the area is excavated, be certain to thoroughly loosen the soil under the bulbs.

Spacing

Space the bulbs according to their ultimate plant size. Instructions are given in the respective bulb sections. In general, large bulbs should be 3-10 inches (7.5-20 cm) apart and small bulbs 1-2 inches (2.5-5.0 cm). If desired, the bulbs that flower at different heights and times can be interplanted in the same area.

Covering and watering the bulbs

After the bulbs are properly spaced cover them using only one-half of the soil that was removed. If the soil is very dry. **Water thoroughly!** Subsequently, finish covering bulbs with remaining soil that was removed and water again. If the fall is dry, water area as needed.

Mulching

The bulb bed should be covered with 2-3 (5-7.5 cm) inches of mulch. This helps to minimize temperature fluctuations and to maintain an optimal moisture level in the bed.

Fertilizer requirements

Fertilization improves performance of spring-flowering bulbs! If a fertilizer program is used, even newly planted bulbs will have improved quality. In addition, fertilization encourages bulbs to perennialize; that is flower for several years without replacing and without digging up the bulbs.

There are 2 fertilizer systems available for spring-flowering bulbs! The first system utilizes a single fall application at planting time. You can purchase "Bulb booster", a combination of sulfur-coated, slow-release and soluble (NPK) fertilizers. This should be incorporated into the rooting area at planting time at a rate of one rounded tablespoon per square foot. The second system uses bone meal incorporated in the rooting area at planting time at a rate of one rounded tablespoon per square foot in combination with an application of 8-8-8 (1 level tablespoon per square foot) in the fall followed by a repeat application of the same fertilizer as soon as the shoots break through the mulch in the spring.

Spring requirements for fall planted bulbs

If 8-8-8 fertilizer was used in fall, repeat the treatment using 1 level tablespoon of 8-8-8 square foot as soon as the shoots break ground in the spring. Do not fertilize spring-flowering bulbs after they have flowered. This tends to encourage the development of bulb rots.

After flower petals fade or fall off, remove flower organs with scissors. Then, allow foliage to die naturally! This permits the bulbs to either increase in size if they are perennial types or to be replaced by flowering sized daughter bulbs if they are replacement types.

Diseases (See Chapter on pages 156-157).

If one starts with healthy bulbs, bulb diseases are generally not a problem. However, if the soil becomes diseased, Terraclor (PCNB) can be incorporated into the bed before planting the bulbs in the fall. The major foliar disease is **Botrytis** (Fire). This disease is controlled by many available fungicides. Check the labels for recommendation or contact your local county extension office.

If the bulbs become heavily infested with viruses, there is no solution except to carefully remove and destroy them.

Insects (See Chapter on pages 156-157).

The primary insect which can become a problem is the aphid and it can be readily controlled by available insecticides. Check the labels for recommendations or contact your local county extension office.

Splitting or harvesting of bulbs

Generally, this is not advised. If the flowering of the bulbs was satisfactory, do not disturb them.

If, however, flowering was unsatisfactory, then remove all the plant tissue (leaves, stems and bulbs) as soon as flowers are finished and replant the area in the fall with new bulbs.

If the bulbs are harvested after the foliage has died and will be replanted in the fall, the bulbs should be stored in open trays or boxes, and preferably at 65-70°F (18-20°C).

PLANTING A DUTCH STYLE FLOWER BED IN THE GRASS.
Store the dug-up ground on a sheet of plastic. The bottom picture shows the height of the blooms in the spring. There were early, middle and late blooming planted.

1/ Dig the ground to a depth of 8 in. (15 cm).

2/ The bulbs are planted after the bottom layer of soil is broken into a fine consistency, possibly with compost or sand worked in.

3/ The bed is refilled with earth.

4/ The ground is lightly raked.
It is possible to overplant with pansies or forget-me-nots.

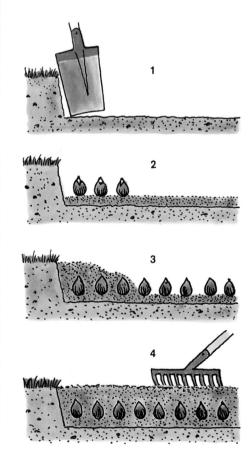

General instructions
Spring-flowering bulbs for southern (climatic zone 8)
and deep south (climatic zone 9) gardens

Most spring-flowering bulbs need an extended period of low temperatures during the winter months to produce a satisfactory flowering response.

There are two classes of spring flowering bulbs for Southern and Deep South gardens. First, there are some bulbs that can be planted in the fall without any special preplanting treatments and which will perform well either as annual or perennial bulbs. Second, there is a group of bulbs that must be given a preplanting cold storage treatment in order for them to perform satisfactorily. These bulbs require 8 to 10 weeks of precooling, i.e. dry cold storage at 40-45° in a refrigerator prior to planting, and then planted in late November and December. A word of caution: When precooling the bulbs in the refrigerator, do not store fruit such as apples, banana's in the same refrigerator. Ripening fruit give off ethylene gas which causes problems with flowering.

One very important aspect for gardeners to consider when planting spring-flowering bulbs in the Deep South is that the bulbs should be planted in an area that does not receive direct sunlight from late morning to late afternoon. This helps to moderate the temperatures. Thus, southern exposures are not highly desirable. As with all other areas, be certain that the area is well-drained and the pH is between 6 and 7. These are always important factors.

Southern gardens (climatic zone 8)

Bulbs listed below generally **do not** need precooling in climatic Zone 8. They should be planted in late November or December.
ALLIUM AFLATUNENSE
ALLIUM CHRISTOPHII
ALLIUM GIGANTEUM
ALLIUM KARTAVIENSE
ALLIUM MOLY
ALLIUM NEAPOLITANUM
ALLIUM SPHAEROCEPHALON
ANEMONE BLANDA
BRODIAEA LAXA
CROCUS
CROCUS CHRYSANTHUS
(snow crocus)
HYACINTHS
DUTCH IRIS
DWARF IRIS
(reticulata)
(danfordiae)
IXIA
MUSCARI ARMENIACUM
(Grape Hyacinth)
MUSCARI BLUE SPIKE
NARCISSUS (do not use double types)
OXALIS ADENOPHYLLA
PUSCHKINIA LIBANOTICA
SCILLA CAMPANULATA
(Wood Hyacinth)
SCILLA SIBERICA
SCILLA TUBERGENIA
TULIPS (Use tall cultivars only)

Note : Some areas of Climatic Zone 8 do not receive 10-12 weeks of winter weather (below 50°F). If you live in such an area, handle the bulbs as escribed for the Deep South Gardens (Climatic Zone 9).

Deep south gardens (climatic zone 9)

Bulbs listed below **do not need** precooling treatment prior to planting in Deep South (Climatic Zone 9).
AMARYLLIS
ALLIUM NEAPOLITANUM
ALLIUM ROSENBACHIANUM
ANEMONE CORONARIA, DE CAEN AND ST. BRIGID
BRODIAEA LAXA "Queen Fabiola"
CROCUS
CROCUS CHRYSANTHUS
(snow crocus)
DUTCH IRIS
IXIAS
NARCISSUS cyclamineus, jonquilla and Triandrus Thalia
PAPERWHITE NARCISSUS
ORNITHOGALUM UMBELLATUM
SCILLA CAMPANULATA (Wood Hyacinth)
SPARAXIS
TRITELEIA UNIFLORA

Bulbs listed below **need** to be precooled before planting in the Deep South (Climatic Zone 9). They should be planted in late November or December.
TULIPS (Use tall cultivars only)
ALLIUMS (other types than listed above)
HYACINTHS
NARCISSUS (Daffodils)
(other types than listed above)
DWARF IRIS (reticulata)
MUSCARIS ARMENIACUM
(Grape Hyacinth)

This group of bulbs should be considered only as annual bulbs. They do not easily perennialize in the Deep South.

It is possible to have a beautiful collection in bloom, indoors, during the winter months.

Home forcing of flowering bulbs

The objective of bulb forcing, whether it is the commercial or amateur forcer, is to have bulbs in flower at times other than when they flower outside under natural environmental conditions. Commercial bulb forcing is a large and important business. Thus, florists can offer a wide range of bulb flowers on almost a year-round basis. There are: Freesias, Dutch Iris, Hyacinths, Narcissi, and Tulips, to name a few. Although commercial forcing is heavily concentrated in The Netherlands, where much of the bulb production occurs, almost every developed country has an established greenhouse for-

cing industry. In the U.S. and Canada, forcers have concentrated on the forcing of bulbs as potted plants. This is the system that is used by homeowners.

Howeowners who want to force bulbs indoors can choose from two basic groups of bulbs. First, there is the traditional group of spring-flowering bulbs that includes tulips, hyacinths, daffodils and some of the smaller bulbs such as CROCUS, MUSCARI and dwarf Iris. All of these are normally forced by planting them in a well-drained planting mix early in the fall and giving them at least 13 weeks of low temperatu-

res below 50°F (10°C) prior to being place in home. This technique is called 'Standard Forcing'! Some of them can also be forced hydroponically (see page 20) by using special glasses or pots and then following the same procedures used for the solid planting mixes. The second group of bulbs that can be forced are the so-called tender bulbs. These bulbs require no low temperatures prior to being placed in the home. The best known are the AMARYLLIS (HIPPEASTRUM) and paperwhite NARCISSUS. The basic guidelines for forcing these 2 groups of bulbs are described in this chapter.

Principal species, cultivars and bulb sizes suitable for forcing

- **Amaryllis (Hyppeastrum)**
  All cultivars can be forced. However, some are best for early forcing, while others are best suited for late forcing.
  Bulb size: Use 26/28 cm in circumference or larger. The flowering plant height and the number of flowers produced will depend on bulb size and the cultivar.

- **Crocus**
  Almost all cultivars can be used, but REMEMBRANCE (Lavender), FLOWER RECORD (Lavender), VICTOR HUGO (Lavender), PICKWICK (Striped), JOAN OF ARC (White), and PETER PAN (White) and LARGE YELLOW are highly adapted to forcing.
  Bulb size: use 9 cm or larger.

- **Dwarf iris**
  IRIS DANFORDIAE and all the IRIS RETICULATA cultivars can be used. Harmony is one of the best.
  Bulb size: Use 6 cm/up.

- **Hyacinths**
  DELFT BLUE and OSTARA (Blue), CARNEGIE (White), and L'INNONCENCE (White), AMSTERDAM (Red), ANNA MARIE (Pink), and PINK PEARL are all highly adapted to forcing.
  Bulb size: Use 17/18 cm and 18/19 cm for earliest forcing and purchase 'Prepared' bulbs. They are the easiest to force.

- **Muscari armeniacum** (Blue)
  MUSCARI are commonly known as Grape Hyacinths.
  Bulb size: Use 9 or 10 cm bulbs.

- **Narcissus** (Large Trumpets)
  DUTCH MASTER (Yellow), EXPLORER (Yellow), GOLDEN HARVEST (Yellow), MT. HOOD (White), and UNSURPASSABLE (Yellow) are highly adapted to forcing.
  Bulb: DN I or DN II size bulbs.

- **Narcissus** (Large-Cupped)
  CARLTON (Yellow), FLOWER RECORD (White with orange cup), ICE FOLLIES (White), YELLOW SUN (Yellow) are highly adapted to forcing.
  Bulb: DN I or DN II size bulbs.

- **Narcissus** (small Cupped)
  BARRETT BROWNING (White with orange cup) is highly adapted to forcing.
  Bulb: DN I or DN II size bulbs.

- **Narcissus** (Double)
  BRIDAL CROWN (White with orange center) is highly adapted to forcing.
  Bulb: DN I or DN II size bulbs.

- **Narcissus cyclamineus**
  FEBRUARY GOLD (Yellow), JACK SNIPE (White with yellow trumpet), PEEPING TOM (Yellow), TETE A TETE (Yellow) are highly adapted to forcing.
  Bulb: DN I or DN II size bulbs.

- **Tulips**
  Red: BING CROSBY, CAPRI, CASSINI, CHARLES, PAUL RICHTER, PROMINENCE, RUBY RED, TRANCE. Pink or Rose: BLENDA, CANTOR, CHRISTMAS MARVEL, GANDER, PRELUDIUM. Yellow: BELLONA, GOLDEN MELODY, KAREOL, MONTE CARLO. White: HIBERNIA, PAX, SNOWSTAR. Lavender: ATTILA, PRINCE CHARLES. Orange: ORANGE MONARCH. Apricot: APRICOT BEAUTY. Bicolors: red and white - LEEN VAN DER MARK, LUCKY STRIKE, MERRY WIDOW, MIRJORAN; red and yellow - ABRA, GOLDEN MIRJORAN, KEES NELIS, THULE.
  Size: Use 12/up cm bulbs.

The cultivars listed above are only a few of the cultivars available for forcing. Others are indicated in the appropriate sections of the book.

Hyacinth 'DELFT BLUE'

Three systems for forcing of bulbs by homeowners

There are three planting media that can be used for home forcing. The most common use is a well-drained soil-based mix. This is used for not only the spring-flowering bulbs that require a cold treatment but also for AMARYLLIS and Paperwhite NARCISSUS. There are a few bulbs that can be forced on water in combination with special containers (see illustrations on page 20). Lastly, paperwhite Narcissus can be forced using gravel as a medium to support the bulbs (see illustration on page 21). Each of these forcing systems is quite easy to use. They key is to follow a few important steps that are required by the bulbs to insure proper growth and development.

Standard forcing of spring-flowering bulbs using a soil-based planting medium

GENERAL INFORMATION
The steps involved in standard forcing spring-flowering bulbs using a well-drained soil mix as a planting medium are simple and are outlined below.

- **First,** the proper cultivars (cultivated varieties) must be selected. This is necessary since all cultivars are not suitable for all flowering periods. The list on this page provides some of the cultivars that are best suited for forcing the most popular species. Some others are indicated in the individual bulb sections.

- **Second,** the bulbs must be planted and given a cold treatment with temperatures ranging from 35° to 48 °F (2-9 °C). This cold treatment can be provided by using either a cold-frame, an unheated cellar or preferably an old home refrigerator. Regardless of the method used, the bulbs must be rooted and cooled for a minimum of 13 weeks. This is needed to insure proper flowering of the species. It is possible to dry cool the bulbs for up to 6 weeks before planting and then root and cool for 9 or more weeks. The main point is that the bulbs receive 13 continuous cold-weeks.

- **Third,** they should be carried into the house for flowering. On the average, the bulbs will take about 3 to 4 weeks to begin flowering. During this time, the homeowner will be able to enjoy a growing plant.

Trumpet narcisses 'CARLTON'

Single early tulip 'CHRISTMAS MARVEL'

MATERIALS

Bulbs

The selection of the proper cultivars for the desired period is highly important. The list on page 18 describes several cultivars which are suitable for pot plant forcings. It is strongly suggested, since some cultivars (see list) may be in short supply, that you place the order with your bulb dealer in the spring to make sure you will have them on time for planting in the fall.

Planting medium

The major purposes of the planting medium are to anchor the bulbs and to hold an adequate moisture supply for the bulbs. Thus, the planting medium must be **well-drained** and yet retain sufficient moisture. A good mixture consists of 1 part loamy soil, 1 part peat, and 1 part sand. Fertilizer should not be added to the mixture.

Containers

Normally 6 or 8 inch (15-20 cm) wide pots are used. Use only clean pots with adequate drainage holes. If the pots have been previously used, scrub and rinse them thoroughly. If they are new plastic pots, be sure that the holes in the bottom of the pot are open. When clay pots are to be used, soak them overnight so they will not draw moisture from the planting medium.

PROCEDURES

Handling of bulbs prior to planting

It is extremely important that flowering bulbs be handled with care at all times. Thet are living plants and should not be dropped or subjected to extreme temperatures. After purchasing, be sure that the bulbs are kept **well-ventilated.** If they come in paper bags, open them to allow maximum air movement. Better yet, store them in open trays. Old strawberry boxes are excellent for this purpose. Keep the bulbs in a room with a temperature between 45° and 55°F (7-13°C). Bulbs can be stored for several weeks at these temperatures. Temperatures above 63°F (17°C) should be avoided at all times.

Planting

Planting can take place any time from October 1 to November 15, depending on the desired date of flowering, the type of storage used, and the prevailing weather. As a general rule, for late flowering, plant late, and for early flowering, plant early. Remember the minimum length of the total cold treatment should be 13 to 14 weeks.

If the bulbs were held dry at 45° to 50°F (7-10°C) (precooled) prior to planting be sure to count this time in the total weeks of cold given. Thus, if bulbs were precooled for 3 weeks they only need 10 weeks more after planting before being brought into the home.

For flowering in late January, the planting must be done around October 1. For February flowering, the bulbs should be planted in mid-October and for March and April, in early-November (except in very cold areas where a mid-October planting is advised).

When planting, (see illustration below) the pot should be loosely filled with enough soil so that the nose (tip) of the bulb will be even with the top of the pot. Place 6 tulips, 3 hyacinths, 6 daffodils, or 15 **Crocus** to 6-inch (15 cm) pot. When planting tulips, you will note that they have a round side and a flat side. Plant them so that the flat side of the bulb will be facing the outside of the pot. When this is done, the first big leaf of the plant will face outward and an attractive pot will be obtained at flowering.

Do not press the bulbs into the soil! The soil under the bulbs should be loose so that good rooting can take place quickly. When covering bulbs, do not overfill the pot. Fill only to within 1/4 inch (0.6 cm) of the top so the plants can be easily watered.

Remember to **label each pot** with the name of the cultivar, date of planting, and date to be placed in the house.

Cold treatment

After planting, three procedures are available for forcing.

The first and by far the best method is to use and old household refrigerator. With it, controlled conditions can be obtained.

A second method is to use a cold storage area such as a vegetable or unheated cellar. As long as the temperatures run between 35-48°F (2-9°C), any type of area can be used successfully. For these methods, it is a good practice to stagger the time of planting as previously suggested. After planting and before placing them in the unheated cellar or refrigerator, **water them well.** A good root system is essential, and this cannot be obtained without proper watering. The bulbs should be watered frequently, making sure that the soil is kept moist.

The third method is to use a cold-frame. The cold-frame should be constructed on a well-drained piece of land and preferably in a shaded area which does not receive heat from the house or direct sunlight. After the pots are placed in the cold-frame, **water them well.** Subsequently, the pots should be covered. There are various covering materials which may be used. These include sand, peat, perlite, sawdust, shredded styrofoam and woodchips. When using a cold-frame, the plantings can be staggered, but remember that the last planting should be done at least 3 weeks prior to hard freezes. If the rains are infrequent, it will be necessary to water to ensure that the pots are kept moist.

Forcing the bulbs

After a minimum of 13 weeks of cold, the first bulbs may be placed in the house. Longer cold storage will result in taller flowers, while storage shorter than 13 weeks will result in smaller plants and they take very long to force. If the first planting was made on October 1, the first plants may be taken into the house right around New Year's Day. For a continuous supply of flowers, bring in a few pots at weekly intervals. In the house, place the plants in an area with a temperature of approximately 60°F (16°C). For best results, place them in direct sunlight. The plants will require about 3 to 4 weeks to flower. Once the flowers begin to color, take them out of the direct sunlight. This helps to prolong the flower life of plants. Since the bulb contains most of the plant food it needs, it is not necessary to fertilize them. If available, however, a solution of $Ca(No_3)_2$ is beneficial when tulips are being forced. Spring-flowering bulbs that have been forced indoors are usually of little value for outdoor plantings. There are, of course, exceptions to this rule and the daffodil is one of them.

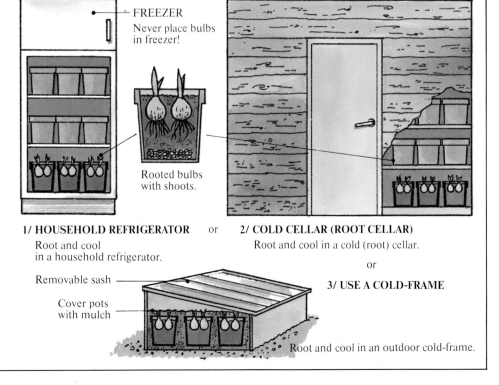

BULB PLANTING FOR FORCING

Step 1
Partially fill pot with soil.

Step 2
Place bulbs with nose even with rim of pot.

Step 3
Cover Bulbs carefully. Fill to about 1/4 inch of pot rim.

FREEZER
Never place bulbs in freezer!

Rooted bulbs with shoots.

1/ HOUSEHOLD REFRIGERATOR   or   **2/ COLD CELLAR (ROOT CELLAR)**

Root and cool in a household refrigerator.

Root and cool in a cold (root) cellar.

or

3/ USE A COLD-FRAME

Removable sash

Cover pots with mulch

Root and cool in an outdoor cold-frame.

Hydroponic forcings

In hydroponic forcings, water replaces the soil-based planting medium. Not all species are suitable for hydroponic forcing. Hyacinths give the best results, although tulips can also be forced with this system. With Hyacinths, usually only one bulb is used. Whereas, with tulips usually 5 bulbs are used. For this type of forcing numerous kinds of pots, both glass and plastic, are available. However, simple jars can be used. The "neck" of the container must be shaped in such a way as to keep the bulb firmly on the water. Also it is absolutely necessary to keep the water just at the base of the bulbs. The roots will take up water and it must be replenished on a periodic basis.

Jingle bells

These unique tulips have the ability to grow in water alone, and they grow extremely fast. Once they are started out in water they develop roots within a week and will bloom within three weeks. Unlike other tulips, they do not need a preplanting treatment of cold or darkness, if the bulbs have been precooled prior to shipping. This does not allow them a long shelf life and it is best to put them on water as soon as they arrive at your home.

It is for this reason that most bulbs of this variety are sold by major mail order houses rather than garden centers or stores. In this way, fast handling and shipping are assured and optimal results can be obtained. 'Jingle Bells' is aptly named since these bulbs are shipped early in December in time to bloom for Christmas.

Hyacinth in glass:
this is the perfect way to let
in the warmth and light.

Hyacinth DELFT BLUE, PINK PEARL and CARNEGIE in translucent glass.

Forcing of Amaryllis

(This information is in presented on page 34)

Narcissus PAPERWHITE in gravel

Crocus REMEMBRANCE in a specially built pot.

Narcissus GRAND SOLEIL D'OR in gravel

Forcing of Paperwhite Narcissus

● FORCING IN CONTAINERS WITHOUT DRAINAGE HOLES

Paperwhites can be forced using decorative containers that do not have drainage holes (see illustration above). To force bulbs using this system, put 1 to 2 inches (2.5-5.0 cm) of washed gravel in the bottom of the container. Carefully place the bulbs on the gravel and subsequently place gravel around the bulbs to hold them in place. Add just enough water to maintain water level at base of the bulbs.

● FORCING IN CONTAINERS WITH DRAINAGE HOLES

Plant in a well-drained pH 6 to 7 sterilized soil-based planting medium. Any size pot can be used. It depends on the number of bulbs purchased. Plant the bulbs with the nose of the bulb either even with or slightly above the rim of the pot. After planting, water thoroughly, then keep the planting medium moist.

● POST PLANTING CONDITIONS IN THE HOME

Paperwhites will flower under any light conditions and usually a 60-65°F (16-18°C) area is best. Initially, a lighted window area is best. When the plants begin to flower, remove them from direct sunlight. No fertilization is required. If healthy bulbs are purchased, no pests are generally encountered.

Landscaping the garden with spring-flowering bulbs

Mixed arrangement using the principal types of bulbs.

Three beds with differently
planted arrangements.

There are no rigid principles for using
spring-flowering bulbs in the landscape. A
major step, however, is planning. As indicated earlier the flowering season for these
bulbs is approximately 4 months long.
There are bulbs for informal borders, formal beds, perennial gardens, wooded areas,
lawns, grassy banks, and rock gardens.
There are a wide range of colors, shapes and
forms available. There are miniature bulbs
and tall majestic ones. Thus, no two gardens will look alike. Everyone can create a
plan for their own enjoyment.
In this chapter, some general advice is given
to aid in planning the garden and to maxi-
mize the enjoyment of the bulbs planted.

Planting in ground beds

Large bed plantings

Flower-bulb beds vary in shape and size. In this
section, we address only the plantings such as
those found in parks, arboreta, and large gardens. These uses of bulbs require close planting
of the bulbs. In most instances, only one species
or cultivar is used. If more than one species or
cultivar are planted, the differences in growing
of the foliage and flowering must be carefully
considered before the bulbs are purchased and
planted. To use large bed plantings one needs a
large garden area. In theory, all bulb species can
be used for this type of planting; however,
tulips, hyacinths and **Narcissus** are most widely
used for large beds.
After flowering, these areas are frequently
replanted with either summer-flowering bulbs,
e.g. Tuberous Begonias or Dahlias, or various
annuals are used. In addition, in some areas, the
beds are overplanted in the fall with plants like
Violets or Pansies in order to give some vegetation and color prior to the flowering of the
bulbs.

Some examples of edge and border planting arrangements.

Borders and mixed borders

Generally, these are irregularly shaped beds and are composed of several kinds of plants. They can, however, be composed of only spring flowering bulbs using different colors, heights, and flowering periods. Mixed borders can be laid out alongside lawns, hedges, and walls. The bulbs can be left in the ground for the whole year or they can be removed and then replaced by other plants after the flowering has been completed. When planning borders, it is essential to take into consideration the heights and spacings needed by different plants. With large bulbs, ten to twelve bulbs of the same cultivar are needed to form an attractive area. For the smaller bulbs, more are needed. The mixed borders normally contain perennial plants. They are known as the famous English or herbaceous borders. Relatively few tall or medium-height perennials flower early in spring. That is why the spring-flowering bulbs are very important additions to the mixed border beds. Tulips, Narcissi, tall Allium's, **Fritillaria imperialis,** and Scilla's are very suitable. After flowering, the dying foliage is obscured by the leaves and flowers of the perennial plants. The bulbs should be left in the ground to perennialize.

Two examples of lower growing bulb types used in rock gardens.

Rock gardens

There are many spring-flowering bulbs that are excellent for use in rock gardens. All the low and medium sized species can be used among low perennial plants. shrubs and small conifers. The season can start with Crocuses, Snowdrops and dwarf Irises **(Iris reticulata and Iris danfordiae).** Later on, dwarf Narcissi, Muscari's, botanical Tulips will flower. These are followed by some of Scilla's, Allium's and **Brodiaea laxa.** Because planting in rock gardens is not always easy, it is essential to choose those bulbs that will perennialize.

Three examples of naturalizing

Other garden uses

It is not always necessary to plant spring-flowering bulbs in planned beds. There are two other uses for these bulbs. First, they can be planted in natural areas such as ground areas, lawns, and open fields or banks and woods. A second use is around the base of trees and shrubs, the leaves of which develop late in spring. They contrast beautifully with early flowering shrubs, e.g. Forsythias, Japanese Quinces, etc. Bulbs like Crocuses, Narcissi, **Anemone blanda,** Scilla's, and **Chionodoxa** do well as naturalized bulbs. These uses are often called "wild" or naturalized plantings. It must be pointed out that the leaves of bulbous species are needed to rebuild the food reserve of the bulbs. Thus, they should not be cut off until they have completely turned yellow.

A nice example of spring flowering

Principal genera, species and cultivars of bulbs

The different forms and colors of all the genera and species described in the book will be given. Most species have numerous, slightly differing cultivars (varieties). All genera are classified alphabetically according to the botanical (Latin) names followed by their English equivalents, the family and when different from the botanical name, the name used in the commercially bulb trade.

For each species, the following important information is provided.
- Flower color and flowering period
- Average plant height
- Planting depth to base of bulb
- Spacing between bulbs
- Light requirements
- Landscape uses

This information is valuable for planning the use of the bulbs either in the landscape or for home forcing.

The terms genus, species, and cultivar (cultivated variety) are often used in this book. Instead of giving a long explanation for these terms an example is given below to provide an understanding of these terms used to classify plants.
Example
TULIPS "QUEEN OF NIGHT"
FAMILY = Liliaceae
GENUS = Tulipa
CLASS = Single late tulip
CULTIVAR (Variety) = Queen of Night

All genera belong to a botanical family. The seven important families for bulbs are:
- Amaryllidaceae
- Araceae
- Iridaceae
- Liliaceae
- Oxalidaceae
- Primulaceae
- Ranunculaceae

Allium

Family: Liliaceae
Common name: ALLIUM'S
OR ORNAMENTAL ONIONS

Origins: Temperate regions of Europe, Asia and the Middle-East. The ornamental Allium's belong to the same family of edible plants that includes garlic, onions, leek and shallots. There are several hundred species, but only about a dozen of them are cultivated to any extent. They offer a diversity of flower colors, heights and forms, and make interesting focal points in the garden. When the foliage, flowers, or bulbs are cut some of them may give a smell of garlic or onion. The smell disappears rapidly when the stems are put in water for a few seconds and this is recommended when they are used as cut flowers. In addition, the flowers of most of the medium and tall species can be used as dry flowers especially after they have been dyed or sprayed. Most of these species flower in early summer, but they are described in this book because they must be planted in fall.

Cultivation

All species and cultivars prefer a well-drained soil. Some require full sunlight and a few require partial shade. Most of them will perennialize to form large and beautiful clumps of flowers. In climatic zones where they do not perennialize, they should be precooled at 40-45°F (5-7°C) for 8-10 weeks before planting in late November.

Principle species

ALLIUM AFLATUNENSE

Flower color and flowering period: Lilac purple, April-May.
Average plant height: 20-30 inches (50-75 cm)
Planting depth to base of bulb: 5 inches (12.5 cm)
Spacing between bulbs: 5 inches (12.5 cm)
Light requirements: Full sun to half-shade.
Landscape uses: beds, borders, perennial beds, cut flowers.

To obtain beautiful results, a minimum of 10 bulbs should be planted. It is one of the best of the ornamental ALLIUM species. The flowers are grouped in dense umbels. The ribbon-like green-blue leaves are very decorative. There are 2 outstanding cultivars: LUCY BALL and PURPLE SENSATION. This species generally perennializes in climatic zones 4-7.

ALLIUM CAERULEUM

Synonym: ALLIUM AZUREUM
Flower color and flowering period: Deep blue, May-June.
Average plant height: 20 inches (50 cm).
Planting depth to base of bulb: 5 inches (12.5 cm)
Spacing between bulbs: 3 inches (5.7 cm).
Light requirements: Full sun.
Landscape uses: Borders, perennial beds, cut flowers.

Species not widely cultivated, but it is available. Does best in climatic zones 5-7.

ALLIUM CHRISTOPHII

synonym: ALLIUM ALBOPILOSUM.
Flower color and flowering period: Silvery-purple, April-June.
Average plant height: 10-20 inches (25-50 cm).
Planting depth to base of bulb: 5 inches (12.5 cm)
Spacing between bulbs: 12 inches (30 cm).
Light requirements: Full sun.
Landscape uses: Borders, perennial beds, cut and dried flowers.

Species has ribbon-like, green-blueish silky and hairy leaves. It has a large umbel that is about 8 inches (20 cm) in diameter with about 80 flowers per umbel. It tends to perennialize in climatic zones 4-8.

ALLIUM KARATAVIENSE

Flower color and flowering period: Lilac to pink, May-June.
Average plant height: 8 inches (20 cm).
Planting depth to base of bulb: 5 inches (12.5 cm)
Spacing between bulbs: 8 inches (20 cm).
Light requirements: Full sun to partial shade.
Landscape uses: Borders and rock gardens.

The leaves are particularly decorative being grey-purple with violet spots. Flowers in very compact umbel on short stems. The flowers have a fragrant smell. Tends to perennialize in climatic zones 4 to 8.

ALLIUM CHRISTOPHII

ALLIUM CAERULEUM

ALLIUM GIGANTEUM

ALLIUM GIGANTEUM

Flower color and flowering period: Purple, May-June.

Average plant height: 34-44 inches (85-110 cm).

Planting depth to base of bulb: 8 inches (20 cm).

Spacing between bulbs: 10 inches (25 cm).

Light requirements: Full sun.

Landscape uses: Perennial gardens, borders, cut and dried flowers.

Plant at least 3 bulbs to get a beautiful effect. It has the name **giganteum** because it is one of the tallest Allium's. The foliage is grey-blueish, curved and strap-like and very decorative, but it usually starts to die by the time the bulb flowers. It has numerous flowers in a 5 inch (12.5 cm) umbel. It tends to perennialize in climatic zones 4 to 8. There is one special cultivar, ROSY GIANT, that is pink or mauve.

ALLIUM MOLY

synonym: ALLIUM LUTEUM

Flower color and flowering period: Bright yellow, May-June.

Average plant height: 10 inches (25 cm).

Planting depth to base of bulb: 5 inches (12.5 cm)

Spacing between bulbs: 3 inches (7.5 cm).

Light requirements: Full sun to partial shade.

Landscape uses: Beds, borders, rock gardens and in ground covers.

It has around a few, long, narrow, green-blueish leaves. Flowers are in loose umbels of about 2 inches (5 cm) in diameter. Tends to perennialize in climatic zones 4-7.

ALLIUM NEAPOLITANUM

Flower color and flowering period: Pure white, April-June.

Average plant height: 15 inches (37.5 cm).

Planting depth to base of bulb: 5 inches (12.5 cm)

Spacing between bulbs: 3 inches (7.5 cm).

Light requirements: Full sun.

Landscape uses: Bed borders, rock gardens and cut flowers.

This species can be cultivated in a conservatory. It is one of the species that has sweet smelling flowers. Flowers are in umbels 2-3 inches (5-7.5 cm) in diameter. It has long narrow, green foliage. It is not a hardy bulb. Thus, is best for climatic zones 7-8. There is one very similar species ALLIUM COWANII that has bigger flowers on 16-20 inches (40-50 cm) stems. There is also a 'Grandiflorum' selection.

ALLIUM OREOPHILUM

synonym: ALLIUM OSTROWSKIANUM

Flower color and flowering period: Red, May-June.

Average plant height: 8 inches (20 cm).

Planting depth to base of bulb: 5 inches (12.5 cm)

Spacing between bulbs: 3 inches (7.5 cm).

Light requirements: Full sun.

Landscape uses: Borders, rock gardens and in ground covers.

It has long and narrow leaves that are blueish-green. Flowers are in umbels that are 3 inches (7.5 cm) in diameter.

ALLIUM PULCHELLUM

Flower color and flowering period: Red-violet, July-August.

Average plant height: 18-22 inches (45-55 cm).

Planting depth to base of bulb: 5 inches (12.5 cm)

Spacing between bulbs: 4 inches (10 cm).

Light requirements: Full sun.

Landscape uses: Borders, cut flowers.

This species is not readily available. It has very interesting pyramidally shaped flowers.

ALLIUM ROSENBACHIANUM

Flower color and flowering period: Lilac purple, April-May.

Average plant height: 30-50 inches (75-125 cm).

Planting depth to base of bulb: 8 inches (20 cm).

Spacing between bulbs: 12 inches (30 cm).

Light requirements: Full sun.

Landscape uses: Perennial beds, borders and cut flowers.

It is one of the tallest of the Allium's. It tends to perennialize in climatic zones 4 to 7. There is a white cultivar A. ROSENBACHIANUM ALBUM.

ALLIUM ROSEUM

Flower color and flowering period: Pink-mauve, June.

Average plant height: 12-16 inches (30-40 cm).

Planting depth to base of bulb: 5 inches (12.5 cm)

Spacing between bulbs: 6-8 inches.

Light requirements: Full sun.

Landscape uses: Small beds, borders, cut flowers.

This species has elegant flowers in umbels on rigid stems. The foliage is green, long and narrow. This species is not readily available.

ALLIUM SPHAEROCEPHALON

Flower color and flowering period: Reddish-purple, May-July.

Average plant height: 15-30 inches (37.5-75 cm).

Planting depth to base of bulb: 5 inches (12.5 cm)

Spacing between bulbs: 3 inches (7.5 cm).

Light requirements: Full sun.

Landscape uses: Borders, perennial beds, cut and dried flowers.

Species has very rigid stems with long narrow green foliage. It tends to perennialize in climatic zones 5-8. It is one of the most reliable species for North America.

ALLIUM STIPITATUM

Flower color and flowering period: Violet-purple, May.

Average plant height: 36-40 inches (90-110 cm).

Planting depth to base of bulb: 5 inches (12.5 cm)

Spacing between bulbs: 8 inches (20 cm).

Light requirements: Full sun.

Landscape uses: Small beds, borders, cut flowers.

This species is not readily available. It has very interesting flowers in large umbels.

ALLIUM SPHAEROCEPHALON

ALLIUM NEAPOLITANUM

ALLIUM OREOPHILUM

ALLIUM KARATAVIENSE.

ALLIUM AFLATUNENSE

Amaryllis

Synonym: HIPPEASTRUM
Family: Amaryllidaceae
Common name: AMARYLLIS

The name, AMARYLLIS, is derived from the name of a Greek shepherdess in the works of the poet Virgil. Although the actual genus of this species is HIPPEAS-TRUM, the name AMARYLLIS, is used because both the bulbs and flowers are commercially sold under this name. One species AMARYLLIS BELLADONNA belongs to the real genus of AMARYLLIS. A. BELLADONNA is related to the other commercial species, but it is more rustic and flowers outdoors in the summer.

There are numerous species of AMARYL-LIS (HIPPEASTRUM). However, the cultivated one was obtained by cross-breeding selections of AMARYLLIS VITTATA (HIPPEASTRUM VITTATUM), which is a native of the tropical and subtropical regions of South America and is itself a hybrid.

Although Amaryllis grow well outside in climatic zones 9 and 10, they are especially adapted for indoor forcing. The Amaryllis is to be considered one of the most elegant and spectacular species to be forced. Amaryllis forcing is very easy and preservation of the bulbs for reflowering requires only a little attention.

Commercially, the Amaryllis is widely cultivated in The Netherlands and South Africa. Depending on the production system and cultivar, it takes three to five years to obtain bulbs large enouth to be offered for sale. The number of flowers and flower stalks produced depends on the size of the bulbs used and the cultivar selected. Normally, the flowers are united in group of four on top of 16-24 inches (40-60 cm) stems, flowering crosswise two by two (see illustrations on pages 35-37). The number of flowers per stalk ranges from 2 to 5. They can have a diameter of 8 inches (25 cm) and there are some minature cultivars with 5 inch (12.5 cm) diameter flowers. The flowers are quite similar in appearance to lilies. The bigger the bulb, the greater the chance that there will be two floral stems with four or more flowers each. Bulbs with a size of 20/24 cm produce one, sometimes two stalks, and 28/up two, and sometimes three floral stalks. Bulb price will depend on the sizes purchased and where it was produced. The second floral stem usually develops after the first one has begun to flower and is often shorter. The long, narrow, supple and curved leaves contrast beautifully with the thick and rigid stalks. The bulbs have several long, fleshy roots and care should be taken not to injure them before planting the bulbs.

A welcome present

Amaryllis are often marketed in attractive boxes with a picture of the cultivar. The boxes can contain the bulb, the pot, and the planting medium necessary for forcing. It is also possible to purchase preplanted bulbs that are ready to force in the home. It is a welcome present especially for those individuals who have little experience in forcing bulbs.

Outdoor planting and cultivation

Outdoors in climatic zones 9 and 10, Amaryllis can be planted either in the fall or in early spring. Depending on the prevailing temperatures, fall planted Amaryllis will flower about 3-4 months after planting. However, when planted outside in April or May, they will flower quicker. When Amaryllis are planted outside they should be fertilized on a monthly basis. Also, if severe cold weather occurs during the winter, the bulbs should be protected against freezing by using a mulch.

Forcing of Amaryllis

Indoor forcing of new or replanted bulbs

Bulbs must be planted in a well-drained (pH 6 to 6.5) sterilized soil-based medium. Use a standard sized 6 inch (15 cm) pot with adequate drainage. Carefully plant the bulb with 1/3 of it being out of the pot (see photograph on right). After planting, water thothoroughly with luke-warm water. Subsequently, keep the medium moist, but not wet. Don't overwater an Amaryllis! Initially grow at 70-75°F (20-23°C) until the bulb begins to root and the leaves and floral stalk begin to grow. Subsequently, any temperature from 65 to 75°F (18-23°C) can be used. In the home, the plant should be kept in a well lighted area **except** when plant is in flower. Then it should be kept out of direct sunlight. Amaryllis tend to grow toward the light. Thus, it is advisable to rotate the pot occasionally. After the plant begins growing, it is necessary to fertilize plant. Use either a complete Nitrogen-Phosphorus-Potassium (NPK) slow release type that lasts for 2-3 months or a liquid (NPK) fertilizer on a 2-4 times per month basis. When all the flowers fade, carefully cut the floral stalk off just above the bulb nose.

The planting and beginning growth of an amaryllis bulb.

Reflowering of the bulb

If the Amaryllis has not lost bulb size or better yet, it has gained in size, it is possible to reflower the bulb. The key is to place the bulb at a temperature of 48-55°F (9-13°C) for a minimum of 8 to 10 weeks during late fall or early winter. This can be accomplished either by stopping watering and placing the bulb in a storage area or by placing the plant in a cool (48-55°F) growing area for this length of time. It is not necessary to let the plant go dormant. Once the plant has received 8-10 weeks of 48-55°F (9-13°C) follow the flowering directions previously given.

Dividing older bulbs

If the bulbs have been grown for 2 or more years, most cultivars will produce one or more offset (daughter) bulblets. Homeowners can handle these older bulbs in 2 ways. First, the bulbs can be transferred to a larger pot with the bulblets left intact. By doing this, ultimately a large number of flowering bulbs will be growing in a single large container. This creates quite a show. Alternatively, the bulblets can be carefully removed and each of them placed in individual pots. Normally, this takes place after the bulbs have been dry stored as described under the reflowering part of this chapter.

Disease and insects

When healthy Amaryllis bulbs are initially purchased, few diseases or insects are encountered. The major disease is STAGONOSPORA commonly known as 'Fire' or 'Red Spot'. The insects that can be encountered are: mites, thrips and mealybugs. If these pests are encountered, contact your local county extension office for advise on pesticides available for use.

Amaryllis in combination with other house plants

If, as a homeowner you have large planters in a hall or atrium, Amaryllis bulbs can be used to enhance the other plants (see illustration on right). Generally, it is best to add them just before they come into flower. However, if the area receives adequate light the bulbs can be forced in the containers. The use of Amaryllis in these types of situations allows the homeowner to use some of their own creativity in producing a colorful setting.

RILONA

WHITE CHRISTMAS

RED LION

Available cultivars:
APPLE BLOSSOM: dark pink on a white background
HERCULES: magenta
LIBERTY: deep red
MINERVA: red, white striped
ORANGE SOUVEREIGN: orange
PICOTEE: pure white, red edges
RED LION: scarlet red
RILONA: salmon pink
WHITE CHRISTMAS: pure white
ZENITH: white, red striped
There are many other cultivars available. This is only a short list and it is intended to illustrate the assortment of colors available.

APPLE BLOSSOM

ORANGE SOUVEREIGN

FAIR LADY

PICOTEE

ZENITH

LIBERTY

MINERVA

Anemone

Family: Ranunculaceae

The name, ANEMONE, is derived from the Greek word Anemos meaning wind. This is a reference to the seeds that are dispersed by the wind.

This genus has about 150 species most of which are herbaceous perennial plants. Of the species cultivated throughout the world, only those that are native to the Mediterranean and Asia Minor are covered in this book.

Principal species
ANEMONE BLANDA

Common Name: GREEK ANEMONES
Flower color and flowering period: white, blue, pink, mauve; March-April.
Average plant height: 4 inches (10 cm).
Planting depth to base of bulb: 5 inches (12.5 cm)
Spacing between bulbs: 2 inches (5 cm).
Light requirements: Full sun or partial shade.
Landscape uses: under shrubs, rock gardens, borders.

The flowers that are about 1 1/2 -2 inches (4-5 cm) in diameter resemble those of the daisies. All of them have a yellow center (see illustrations on right). This species should be left in the in the ground and tends to perennialize in climatic zones 4-7. When they do perennialize, they form beautiful flower carpets. In the spring, they flower under trees and ornamental shrubs and their pastel shades combine beautifully with crabapple trees and weeping cherry trees. These trees and shrubs do not have leaves in March-April and they permit ANEMONE BLANDA to make a magnificent display of the delicate long lasting colors.

Principal cultivars
ANEMONE BLANDA comes in a mix of various flower colors. There are the named species and cultivars listed below that provide a single color.
ATROCAERULEA (INGRAMII): dark violet-blue
BLUE SHADES: light to dark blue shades
PINK STAR: pink
RADAR: deep rose
MIXED COLORS: mixed colors
WHITE SPLENDOUR: pure white.

ANEMONE BLANDA mixed

ANEMONE BLANDA "WHITE SPLENDOUR".

ANEMONE BLANDA "RADAR"

ANEMONE BLANDA "BLUE SHADES"

ANEMONE CORONARIA

Common Name: FLORIST'S ANEMONE
Flower color and flowering period: white, light and deep blue, pink, red, or mauve; April-May.
Average plant height: 8 inches (20 cm).
Planting depth to base of bulb: 5 inches (12.5 cm)
Spacing between bulbs: 3 inches (7.5 cm).
Light requirements: Full sun or partial shade.
Landscape uses: beds, borders, rock gardens, cut flowers.

Commercially, A. CORONARIA is widely cultivated for use as a cut-flower. Hence, its name Florist's Anemone. The vivid colors make marvelous bouquets. The flowers, 2 inches (5 cm) in diameter, are characterized by a preeminent black heart, surrounded by a white or cream corolla separating it from the predominate color of the petals (see illustrations on pages 40-41). Long stamens surround the center and the relatively few leaves are delicately divided.

This species is not very hardy. They should be planted in a protected area of the garden and mulched for the winter months. They prefer a fertile and well-drained soil. This Anemone can be planted either in the fall in warm areas (Climatic Zones 8-10) or in the spring in colder areas (Climatic Zones 4-7), where they will flower about three or four months after planting. Before planting, the bulbs should be soaked in luke-warm water for 24 hours. The shoots develop from the eyes on top of the bulb, so try to plant the bulb upright. It is sometimes difficult to see the eyes since they are surrounded by brown, small scales. If, however, the bulb is planted upside down, the shoots will turn upright and the main effect is that flowering is lightly delayed. Because this Anemone has a large root system, the planting distance should be at least 3 inches (7.5 cm) between bulbs. The bulbs can be left in the ground, however, the flowers tend to become smaller rather quickly. Thus, they should be replaced every couple years.

Principal cultivars
ANEMONE DE CAEN (single flowers)
A MIXED ASSORTMENT OF COLORS IS SOLD. Also, there are named cultivars.
Mr. FOKKER: violet-blue
SYLPHIDE: violet-rose
THE BRIDE: white
ANEMONE ST. BRIGID (semi-double flowers)
Common Name: ANEMONE SAINT BRIGID, patron saint of Ireland.
A MIXED ASSORTMENT OF COLORS IS SOLD. Also, there are named cultivars.
HOLLANDIA (His Excellency): scarlet
LORD LIEUTENANT: deep blue
MOUNT EVEREST: pure white
ROYAL PURPLE: purple-violet
THE ADMIRAL: violet
THE GOVERNOR: scarlet-red.

ANEMONE FULGENS (St. Bavo)

Flower color and flowering period: scarlet red; March-May.
Average plant height: 8 inches (20 cm).
Planting depth to base of bulb: 5 inches (12.5 cm)
Spacing between bulbs: 3 inches (7.5 cm).
Light requirements: Full sun or partial shade.
Landscape uses: borders, beds, rock gardens and cut flowers.

ANEMONE FULGENS is related to ANEMONE DE CAEN. The flowers are as big as those of ANEMONE DE CAEN, but the petals are more oval. Flowers are scarlet-red and the green leaves are beautifully divided. It requires a well drained soil. It does not tend to perennialize.

Specialists in rare bulbs also offer: ANEMONE APENNINA which is blue, and ANEMONE NEMOROSA, which is white. They are closely related to ANEMONE BLANDA.

ANEMONE FULGENS

ANEMONE DE CAEN
mixed

ANEMONE ST. BRIGID mixed

ANEMONE FULGENS "SAINT BAVO"

ANEMONE DE CAEN and ST. BRIGID combined with other bulb types.

41

Arum Italicum

Family: Araceae
Common name: ARUM OF ITALY

ARUM ITALICUM grows readily on the coast of the Mediterranean. It does not flower prolifically. The veined and marbled leaves are very decorative and generally they come up in the fall and then persists through the winter.

Planting and cultivation
Flower color and flowering period: Green, May.
Average plant height: Floral stems are 20-24 inches (50-60 cm) tall and foliage is 12-16 inches (30-40 cm) long.
Planting depth to base of bulb: 5 inches (12.5 cm)
Spacing between bulbs: 12 inches (30 cm)
Landscape uses: In perennial beds, under trees and shrubs, and as cut flowers.

Prefers a very moist soil. In May, the long spathes appear a pale green-yellow. Bunches of **toxic,** bright orange fruits will follow. The green foliage, white veined, persists through winter and until about June. It is this characteristic that makes the plant interesting, because decorative foliage of bulbs during the winter is not too common.

ARUM ITALICUM – leaf   flower   seed pod

Brodiaea laxa

synonym: TRITELEIA LAXA
Family: Liliaceae
Common name: BRODIAEA

An important, but very complex genus. There are species many of whom are considered to be in various genera. They include: BREVOORTIA, DICHELOSTEMMA, IPHEION, and TRITELEIA.
BRODIAEA LAXA and particularly the selection 'Queen Fabiola', is the only species that is widely cultivated and available.
Flower color and flowering period: Blue and white; May-July.
Average plant height: 14-16 inches (35-40 cm).
Planting depth to base of bulb: 5 inches (12.5 cm)
Spacing between bulbs: 3 inches (7.5 cm)
Light requirements: Full sun to partial shade.
Landscape uses: beds, borders, rock gardens, ground covers, fields, and cut-flowers.
Brodiaea is not very winter hardy. It should be planted in a well-drained soil and in a sheltered place. In winter, the area should be protected with a mulch. It tends to perennialize in climatic zones 5 to 9 and will grow into beautiful clumps. The flowers are united in an umbel on top of strong stems. The foliage is rather sparse.

Available cultivars:
QUEEN FABIOLA: big flowers, intense blue-mauve
CANDIDA: pure white.

BRODIAEA LAXA "QUEEN FABOLIA"

Bulbocodium vernum

synonym: COLCHICUM VERNUM; COLCHICUM BULBOCODIUM
Family: Liliaceae
Common name: RED CROCUS

Flower color and flowering period: Deep Rose, February-March.
Average plant height: 4-5 inches (10-12.5 cm).
Planting depth to base of bulb: 5 inches (12.5 cm)
Spacing between bulbs: 3 inches (7.5 cm)
Light requirements: Full to partial shade.
Landscape uses: rock gardens, under trees and shrubs, and perennial beds.
Species is closely related to CROCUS and COLCHICUM, but the flowers are much longer and the petals spread apart, specially as the plant ages (see photograph on page 43). The small and purple leaves become long and green. Each bulb has two or three flowers and three leaves. BULBOCODIUM grows best in well drained soils and prefers to remain in the ground, where it naturalizes.

Camassia

Family: Liliaceae
Common names: Edible CAMASSIA
and Indian Quamash

The name is derived from Quamash, an Indian word. This genus has 7-8 bulbous species. It is native to western North America where it grows in the wild in the mountains and on the prairies. Although the bulbs, the stems and leaves are poisonous, the Indians ate the bulbs of certain species after cooking them. At present, three species are cultivated and they deserve to be better-known and used. The plants have a wild appearance but the flowers are striking. Generally, Camassia's are offered only by firms specialized in rare or unusual bulbs.

Cultivation

Camassia's grow best in well drained soils. They prefer to remain in the ground and will naturalize in climatic zones 5 to 7. If they become too thick, they should be divided in early fall. All species flower at the end of spring.

Principal species

CAMASSIA CUSICKII

Flower color and flowering period: light blue; May.
Average plant height: 20 inches (50 cm).
Planting depth to base of bulb: 5 inches (12.5 cm)
Spacing between bulbs: 4 inches (10 cm)
Light requirements: Full to partial shade.
Landscape uses: beds, borders, cut flowers, fields, ground covers, and rock gardens.
The species has green, narrow and rigid leaves. The flowers are borne on long spikes.

CAMASSIA ESCULENTA

synonym: CAMASSIA, QUAMASH
Flower color and flowering period: Deep Blue, May-June.
Average plant height: 16 inches (40 cm).
Planting depth to base of bulb: 5 inches (12.5 cm)
Spacing between bulbs: 3 inches (7.5 cm).
Light requirements: Full to partial shade.
Landscape uses: beds, borders, cut flowers, fields, ground covers and rock gardens.
The Indians ate the bulbs of this species.

CAMASSIA LEICHTLINII

Flower color and flowering period: White, violet-purple, yellow; May-June.
Average plant height: 28-36 inches (70-90 cm).
Planting depth to base of bulb: 5 inches (12.5 cm)
Spacing between bulbs: 3 inches (7.5 cm).
Light requirements: Full sun to partial shade.
Landscape uses: beds, borders, cut flowers, fields, ground covers and rock gardens.
This is an excellent species, rapidly developing into compact groups. Flowers are closely borne on spikes of 6-8 inches (15-20 cm). One variety: "Flore Plena" has double, sulphur-yellow flowers.

CAMASSIA CUSICKII

CAMASSIA ESCULENTA dark blue

BULBOCODUM VERNUM

CAMASSIA LEICHTLINII

CAMASSIA ESCULENTA light blue

Chionodoxa

Family: Liliaceae.
Common name: CHIONODOXA'S,
GLORY-OF-THE-SNOW.

There are relatively few species of CHIONO-DOXA. Most of them are native to Asia Minor, Crete and Cyprus. They are amongst the first bulbs to flower in the spring. They are very strong and grow well in almost all type soils. They tend to perennialize in climatic zones 4 to 7. The foliage is quite similar to that of the Dutch hyacinths.
Flower color and flowering period: Light and dark blues with white centers, March-April.
Average plant height: 4-5 inches (10-12.5 cm).
Planting depth to base of bulb: 5 inches (12.5 cm)
Spacing between bulbs: 2 inches (5 cm).
Light requirements: Full sun to partial shade.
Landscape uses: borders, rock gardens, and under trees and shrubs.
Where they perennialize, the bulbs should be left in the ground.

Principal varieties

CHIONODOXA GIGANTEA
synonym: CHIONODOXA GRANDIFLORA
Height: 4 inches (10 cm).
This species is one of the most important ones available. Flowers are pale blue, about 1-1/2 inches (3-5 cm) in diameter, with a white eye in the center.

CHIONODOXA LUCILIAE
Height: 4 inches (10 cm).
Brilliant light blue flowers, about 1 inch (2.5 cm) in diameter, with a very white center (see photograph below). Owes its name to the Swiss botanist E. Bossier who discovered it in Asia Minor and named it after his wife Lucile. There are cultivars with different colors, but they are not often cultivated.
ALBA: white flowers.
PINK GIANT: big flowers, bright pink.
ROSEA: tender pink.

CHIONODOXA SARDENSIS
Height: 4 inches (10 cm).
It is very close to the other species and has blue-mauve flowers with white centers (see photograph below). Contrary to what its name suggests, it is native to the plains of Sardisen in Turkey and not to Sardinia.

Corydalis solida

Family: Papaveraceae
synonym: FUMARIA BULBOSA

The genus consists of some 100 annual, perennial or bulbous species, but only the bulbous CORYDALIS SOLIDA is cultivated.
Flower color and flowering period: Pink-purple, April-May.
Average plant height: 6-8 inches (15-20 cm).
Planting depth to base of bulb: 5 inches (12.5 cm)
Spacing between bulbs: 5 inches (12.5 cm).
Light requirements: partial shade.
Landscape uses: rock gardens, and under shrubs and trees.
The pink-purple flowers are borne in elegant racemes. The foliage is green-bluish and is sharply divided. The bulbs require a well drained soil and prefer to remain in the ground in order to perennialize.

CHIONODOXA LUCILIAE

CHIONODOXA GIGANTEA

CHIONODOXA SARDENSIS

Crocus

CROCUS CHRYSANTHUS "ZWANENBURG BRONZE"

Crocus

Family: Iridaceae

The name CROCUS is derived from Greek word Krokos. This genus consists of more than 100 species of which about 30 are cultivated. However, only 5 are commercially important. Together with Hyacinths, Daffodils (NARCISSUS) and Tulips they are among the most popular bulbs used in the landscape. There are some species that are planted in the summer and flower in the fall. They will be described in another book. CROCUS should not be confounded with COLCHIUM, a different species, that has similar flowers. The spring-flowering species are native to the mountainous regions of the Mediterranean. CROCUS have a long history of cultivation.

Planting and cultivation

Flower color and flowering period: Yellow, white, purple, striped and bronze; February-March.
Average plant height: 3-5 inches (7.5-12.5 cm).
Planting depth to base of bulb: 5 inches (12.5 cm)
Spacing between bulbs: 1 inches (2.5 cm).
Light requirements: Full sun to partial shade.
Landscape uses: borders, rock gardens, in lawns, under shrubs and trees and for forcing (See Chapter on Forcing).
CROCUS require a well drained soil. They prefer to remain in the soil where they, perennialize, (climatic zones 4 to 8) and form beautiful clumps. When CROCUS perennialize they flower earlier than newly planted bulbs. Beautiful combinations can be obtained with other small bulbs or perennial plants that have the same early period of flowering. The flowers of all species are chalice-shaped. They close at night and in bad weather and open when the sun shines. The foliage is green and long with silver grey streaks. The stigmas of the flower are very colorful.

Principal species

CROCUS ANCYRENSIS
Common name: CROCUS "GOLDEN BUNCH"
Flowering: golden yellow; February-March
Height: 4 inches (10 cm)

CROCUS CHRYSANTHUS
(Snow crocus)
Common name: BOTANICAL CROCUS
Flowering: February-March
Height: 3 inches (7.5 cm)
Has more but smaller flowers than the better-known CROCUS VERNUS (DUTCH CROCUS). Flowers often bi-colored with a yellow-orange heart. Range of colors is more varied than that of CROCUS VERNUS. The bulbs are also smaller.

Principal cultivars
CREAM BEAUTY: cream yellow.
BLUE BIRD: tender blue outside, cream inside.
BLUE PEARL: bright blue outside, white inside.
BRONZE BEAUTY: yellow and bronze purple outside.
E. A. BOWLES: golden yellow.
FUSCOTINCTUS: bronze, violet-striped.
HERALD: yellow with brown flushes.
LADYKILLER: blue-violet, white veined, inside yellow.
SATURNUS: golden-yellow, brown-purple striped light blue with darker acc.
SKYLINE: deep blue, striped white.
SNOWBUNTING: pure white, outside purple-violet veined, orange base.
ZWANENBURG BRONZE: bronze, outside yellow striped, inside golden yellow. One of the most spectacular varieties.
Mixtures of many of the cultivars are also sold.

CROCUS CHRYSANTHUS "FUSCOTINCTUS "

CROCUS CHRYSANTHUS "LADYKILLER "

CROCUS CHRYSANTHUS "SNOWBUNTING "

CROCUS CHRYSANTHUS "SATURNUS "

CROCUS CHRYSANTHUS "BLUE PEARL "

CROCUS CHRYSANTHUS "CREAM BEAUTY"

CROCUS SIEBERI
"HUBERT EDELSTEN"

CROCUS CHRYSANTHUS "BRONZE BEAUTY"   CROCUS CHRYSANTHUS "BLUE BIRD"   CROCUS CHRYSANTHUS "HERALD"

CROCUS TOMASINIANUS "RUBY GIANT"

CROCUS SIEBERI

CROCUS FLAVUS

synonym: CROCUS LUTEUS
Flowering: Yellow; March-April.
Height: 4 inches (10 cm).
Quite similar to CROCUS VERNUS, but the golden yellow flowers are a little smaller. It is also known as 'large yellow' or 'yellow mammoth'.

CROCUS SIEBERI

Flowering: Blue with yellow center; March-April
Height: 3 inches (7.5 cm).
A vigorous species. The flowers are light blue with a yellow center and bright red-orange stigmas. "Hubert EDELSTEN" (page 48) is a hybrid with white feathering.

CROCUS TOMASINIANUS

Flowering: Lavender; March-April.
Height: 3 inches (7.5 cm).
All cultivars have lavender flowers. When they open, the six petals form a star. CROCUS TOMASINIANUS naturalizes very easily.

Principal cultivars:
Three beautiful varieties are cultivated;
BARR'S PURPLE
RUBY GIANT
WHITEWELL PURPLE

CROCUS FLAVUS

CROCUS VERNUS "REMEMBRANCE"

CROCUS VERNUS "VANGUARD"

CROCUS VERNUS planted in clusters

CROCUS VERNUS

Common name: DUTCH CROCUS
Flowering: February-April
Height: 4 inches (10 cm).

This is the most widely cultivated species. Over several centuries the cultivars have been obtained by selection and cross breeding from the wild species, crocus. Generally, the flowers are bigger than those of the other species. They grow well in lawns, contrasting beautifully with the green grass. It is important, however, to be certain not to cut the leaves off when the lawn is mowed. The leaves are needed for photosynthesis to build up the new bulbs for the next season.

Principal varieties:
FLOWER RECORD: shining violet-mauve
GRAND MAITRE: lavender-violet
JOAN OF ARC: pure white
PETER PAN: pure white
PICKWICK: very pale blue, striped white
PURPUREUS GRANDIFLORUS: violet purple
QUEEN OF THE BLUES: deep blue with lighter margin
REMEMBRANCE: deep blue-violet (the best cultivar for indoor forcing)
VANGUARD: light lavender
CROCUS VERNUS are also sold in mixtures.

CROCUS VERNUS "QUEEN OF THE BLUES"

CROCUS FLAVUS "YELLOW MAMMOUTH"

CROCUS VERNUS "PICKWICK"

CROCUS VERNUS "JOAN OF ARC"

CROCUS VERNUS 'FLOWER RECORD'

Cyclamen

Family: Primulaceae

This genus consists of about fifteen species that are native to the Mediterranean region. The most popular is the famous CYCLAMEN PERSICUM, commonly known as Cyclamen of Persia or Florist's Cyclamen. From this species many hybrids with different colors and shapes have been raised. Commercially, it can be purchased throughout the year since it is grown in greenhouses.

Principal species

Three species have been cultivated from the bulbs and being quite similar it is difficult to distinguish between them.
* CYCLAMEN EUROPAEUM
(Cyclamen of Europe)
* CYCLAMEN NEAPOLITANUM
(Cyclamen of Naples)
* CYCLAMEN COUM
(Cyclamen of the Isle of Cos)
CYCLAMEN COUM is the only species flowering in spring and that is why the other two are not described in this book.

CYCLAMEN COUM

syn. CYCLAMEN IBERICUM,
C. VERNUM or C. ORBICULATUM
Flower color and flowering period: purple-violet, pink or white; December-March.
Average plant height: 4 inches (10 cm).
Planting depth to base of bulb: 4 inches (12.5 cm)
Spacing between bulbs: 4 inches (10 cm).
Light requirements: Partial shade.
Landscape uses: rock gardens and under trees and shrubs.

This species requires fertile, well-drained soil and, where it is hardy prefers, to be left in the ground. Each year a layer of leafmold compost is necessary for good growth. The small green, ground leaves are silver-cream veined and on the reverse side hairy and purple. The flowers are about 1 inch (2.5 cm) wide on rigid stems (see photograph on right).

CYCLAMEN COUM, mixed

Dracunculus vulgaris

Family: Araceae
Common Name: DRACUNCULUS
and Serpentine Dragon

The two species, DRACUNCULUS VULGARIS and DRACUNCULUS CANARIENSIS, grow wild in Europe. They are not widely used and they are frequently confused with ARUM.

Planting and cultivation
Flower color and flowering period: Reddish-brown with a green base; May-June.
Average plant height: 20 inches (50 cm).
Planting depth to base of bulb: 6 inches (15 cm).
Spacing between bulbs: 12 inches (30 cm).
Light requirements: Full sun.
Landscape uses: fields and borders.
DRACUNCULUS are semi-hardy bulbs. They do best in climatic zones 7-9. Grows easily in all soils, but prefers a fertile, well-drained soil. Plants should not be watered in summer and in the winter they should be protected with a mulch. The leaves are deeply lobed, white-striped, and develop in spring. The reddish-brown flowers with a green base can be 18 inches (50 cm) long and 8 inches (20 cm) wide. A few days after the flowers are completely open, they have a smell of rotting flesh and this attracts flies. Therefore, they should not be planted near the home.

DRACUNCULUS VULGARIS

Eranthis

Family: Ranunculaceae
Common names: ERANTHIS,
Winter Aconite

Name derived from Greek ER (spring) and Anthos (flower). ERANTHIS is native to the mountainous region of Europe and Asia. There are 7-8 species, but only three of them are cultivated commercially. They are all quite similar in most aspects and in their cultivation.

Planting and cultivation

Flower color and flowering period: yellow; March-April.
Average plant height: 3 inches (7.5 cm).
Planting depth to base of bulb: 5 inches (12.5 cm)
Spacing between bulbs: 2 inches (5 cm).
Light requirements: Full sun to partial shade.
Landscape uses: borders, rock gardens and under trees and shrubs.
ERANTHIS prefers a well-drained soil. Bulbs are very small and look like pieces of bark. Prior to planting, soak them in luke-warm water for 24 hours. This facilitates the development of the plant. Their flowers, among the first in spring, and they often appear in the snow. With their lively yellow flowers, they look like buttercups (see photographs on page 53). The flowers are borne on very short stems. Flowers will open in full sun and close again at night or when there is no sunshine. The green leaves form a little collar around the flower. When the flowers fade they form a green carpet which disappears at the end of spring.

Principal species

ERANTHIS CILICICA

Eranthis of Sicily.
Average Plant Height: 3 inches (7.5 cm).
It has big flowers that are bright yellow, and it flowers in March or early April. The foliage is green-bronze. It is a vigorous species.

ERANTHIS HYEMALIS

Height: 3 inches (7.5 cm).
Flowers are lemon-yellow. It is smaller than E. CILICICA. It also flowers in March or early April. The foliage has pale blue cast and is highly lobed. It is a well-known species.

ERANTHIS TUBERGENII

Average plant height: 4 inches (10 cm).
A hybrid from the two former species raised by the Dutch firm Van Tubergen. It is more robust, has bigger flowers, and flowers a little later.

ERANTHIS CILICICA

ERANTHIS HYEMALIS

ERANTHIS HIEMALIS and IRIS RETICULATA in melting snow

Eremurus

Name is derived from the Greek words ERE-MOS meaning solitary and OURA meaning tall.

They are native to Asia. Eremurus is a very spectacular plant. There are 30-40 species, of which three are cultivated commercially. These plants are not widely used in the garden, but deserve more consideration.

Planting and cultivation

Flowering period: May-July.
Average plant height: 30-70 inches (75-175 cm), depending on the species or cultivar.
Planting depth to base of bulb: 5 inches (12.5 cm)
The species has long and thick tuberous roots. When they are planted, the roots should be carefully spread out. In a relatively heavy soil, the roots must be surrounded by sand and the central bud barely covered with sand.
Spacing between bulbs: 12-24 inches (30-60 cm).
Light requirements: Full sun.
Landscape uses: At the back of borders and perennial beds. They are excellent cut flowers.
EREMURUS prefers a light, sandy and fertile soil. In regions with severe winters and spring, they should be planted in a sheltered spot in the garden. Although the bulbs are hardy, they must be protected from severe cold in winter and the use of mulch is advised. Kept in the ground for 3-4 years, they develop into beautiful clumps. Each year some fertilizer must be added to the soil to guarantee good growth. From May onwards long and rigid stems grow from a rosette of long, supple, narrow and shining green leaves. The abundant small flowers are borne on spikes which can be as long as 70 inches (175 cm). Colors are: white, yellow, pink, salmon, and bright orange.

Principal species

EREMURUS BUNGEI

synonym: EREMURUS STENOPHYLLUS.
This is the smallest species with a maximum height of 50 inches (125 cm).
Flowers are golden-yellow in June-July. It is native to Turkestan and Afghanistan.

EREMURUS ROBUSTUS

This species has a maximum height of 70 inches (175 cm).
Flowers are very pale pink and it usually flowers in June.

EREMURUS
'Ruiter and Shelford hybrids'

Their average height is about 40 inches (100 cm). They have a beautiful range of pastel (salmon-yellow-orange) flowers. These are amongst the most widely available Eremurus.

EREMURUS HIMALAICUS

Flowers are white and it usually flowers in May or early June.

EREMURUS ROBUSTUS   EREMURUS BUNGEI

Erythronium Revolutum "PAGODA"

Erythronium Dens-Canis "PURPLE KING"

Erythronium Dens-Canis "LILAC WONDER"

Erythronium

Common names: Dog's-Tooth-Violet, Trout-Lily, Adders-Tongue
Family: Liliaceae.

This genus consists of about fifteen species that are native to North America. There is one species native to Central Europe, Asia across to Japan, ERYTHRONIUM DENS-CANIS. It is commonly known as 'Dog's Tooth Violet' and grows in the wild in the woods of mountainous regions. The name of Dog's Tooth referred to the shape of the bulb.

Planting and cultivation

Flower color and flowering period: Yellow or white; March-April.
Average plant height: 10 inches (25 cm).
Planting depth to base of bulb: 5 inches (12.5 cm)
Spacing between bulbs: 3 inches (7.5 cm).
Light requirements: Full or partial shade.
Landscape uses: under trees and shrubs, well drained rock gardens and perennial beds.
ERYTHRONIUM requires a fertile soil that must retain moisture. It prefers to be left in the ground to form beautiful clumps flowering in spring for a great many years. During dry summers, a layer of mulch is useful to help retain moisture in the soil.

Principal species

There are two species and their hybrids that are cultivated commercially.

ERYTHRONIUM DENS-CANIS

Derived from the wild species it has bright pink flowers and brilliant green, brown-spotted decorative foliage. Some hybrids have been developed from this species (see photographs on right).
Flowering period: April-May.
Average plant height: 6-8 inches (15-20 cm).
The most beautiful hybrids are:
Lilac Wonder: Lilac.
Purple King: deep purple with white heart.
White Splendour: pure white.

ERYTHRONIUM REVOLUTUM

WHITE BEAUTY
White flowers with brown basal spots, average plant height is 8-10 inches (20-25 cm). It has decorative, spotted foliage. By cross-breeding ERYTHRONIUM REVOLUTUM and ERYTHRONIUM TUOLUMNENSE two hybrids have been obtained:
KONDO
Bright yellow flowers with brown rings. Leaves have bronze-colored spots. Average Plant Height: 10-12 inches (25-30 cm).
PAGODA
Golden-yellow flowers with brown hearts. Bronze-colored ans spotted leaves. Averager Plant Height: 10-12 inches (25-30 cm). Abundant flowering, each stem having 5-6 flowers. This is one of the best of the hybrids (see photograph above).

Erythronium Revolutum "WHITE BEAUTY"

Fritillaria

Family: Liliaceae

The genus FRITILLARIA consists of numerous species that differ greatly one from another. Only five of them are cultivated and three of them have outstanding landscape uses.

Principal species

FRITILLARIA ACMOPETALA

It is native to Asia Minor and is highly desired by collectors of rare bulbs.

Flower color and flowering period: greenish-yellow, brown-violet spotted; April.

Average plant height: 16-20 inches (40-50 cm).

Planting depth to base of bulb: 5 inches (12.5 cm)

Spacing between bulbs: 4 inches (10 cm).

Light requirements: Full sun to partial shade.

Landscape uses: beds, borders, rock gardens, and under trees and shrubs.

Flowers are bell-shaped with two or three on one stem (see photographs on page 57). Leaves are sparse and narrow.

FRITILLARIA IMPERIALIS

Common name: CROWN IMPERIAL

This is one of the best-known species. In addition, it is also one of the oldest bulbs cultivated and it is native to Asia and the Middle East.

Flower color and flowering period: yellow, orange-red, red; April-May.

Average plant height: 18-24 inches (45-60 cm).

Planting depth to base of bulb: 8 inches (20 cm).

Spacing between bulbs: 12 inches (30 cm).

Light requirements: Full sun to partial shade (particularly in warmer climatic zones).

Landscape uses: perennial beds and borders.

Should be planted as early as possible in the fall. Requires a well-drained, but rather poor and dry soil. It is recommended to plant the bulbs in a layer of sand or on slope to ensure a minimum of moisture.

Due to its delicate nature, FRITILLARIA IMPERIALIS prefers to be kept in the ground. It grows well and multiplies best in climatic zones 4 to 6. After flowering and complete drying of the leaves, the stems should be cut off just above the ground. Mark the location of the bulbs to avoid any damage when digging, raking, etc.

The flowers have a musky smell and anytime you touch the flower, it drops a tear.

Principal cultivars:

AURORA: orange-red
(see photograph above).

LUTEA: bright yellow
(see photograph above).

RUBRA: deep vermillion red.

RUBRA MAXIMA: very big flowers, deep vermillion red.

FRITILLARIA MELEAGRIS

Common names: Snake's Head FRITILLA-RIA, Guinea Hen Flower.

F. MELEAGRIS is totally different from F. IMPERIALIS. It is a native to Europe where it is often found in peat and high organic soils.

Flower color and flowering period: purple or white; April-May.

Average plant height: 10 inches (25 cm).

Planting depth to base of bulb: 5 inches (12.5 cm)

Spacing between bulbs: 2 inches (5 cm).

Light requirements: Full sun to partial shade.

Landscape uses: borders, rock gardens, lawns, under trees and shrubs, and perennial beds.

This species prefers a fairly moist soil. Thus, the incorporation of peat into the soil is advised. The bulbs should be left in the ground and the leaves should be cut off only after they have turned completely yellow. The bell-shaped flowers grow on stems, with 5-6 narrow, bluish-green leaves (see photograph below). They are usually sold in mixed colors, but some cultivars are available by specialists.

Principal varieties
APHRODITE: pure white
CHARON: reddish-brown
POMONA: white checkered pink
POSEIDON: white, checkered purple, big flowers on smaller stems.
Generally, a mixture is offered for sale.

FRITILLARIA PERSICA

Common name: FRITILLARIA OF PERSIA.

Flower color and flowering period: deep purple-violet; April-May.

Average plant height: 30 inches (75 cm).

Planting depth to base of bulb: 5 inches (12.5 cm)

Spacing between bulbs: 8 inches (20 cm).

Light requirements: Full sun.

Landscape uses: perennial beds and borders.

Requires the same cultivation as FRITILLA-RIA IMPERIALIS (Crown Imperial). The two species are often planted together. The bell-shaped flowers are borne on strong stems and have a delicious smell. The bright green and narrow leaves grow on the stems in a regular pattern. They form interesting compositions with white or yellow NARCISSUS (Daffodils), contrasting beautifully with their deeper shades of color.

FRITILLARIA PONTICA

This little-known species is native to Asia Minor and Southeastern Europe.

Flower color and flowering period: greenish, spotted brown and orange; May-June.

Average plant height: 16 inches (40 cm).

Planting depth to base of bulb: 5 inches (12.5 cm)

Spacing between bulbs: 4 inches (10 cm).

Light requirements: Full or partial shade.

Landscape uses: rock gardens and under trees and shrubs.

The bell-shaped solitary flowers have a disagreeable smell.

FRITILLARIA PONTICA

FRITILLARIA PERSICA

FRITILLARIA MELEAGRIS

Galanthus

Common name: SNOWDROP
Family: Amaryllidaceae.

This genus consists of dozen species that are
native to Asia Minor and Europe.
All of them have white flowers, but foliage and
flowering-periods are different.

Principal varieties

Two species are cultivated. However, GALAN-
THUS NIVALIS, the common 'Snowdrop', is
one of the most popular and earliest spring flowering bulbs.

GALANTHUS NIVALIS (Snowdrop)

GALANTHUS NIVALIS and ERANTHIS make good neighbors

GALANTHUS ELWESII

Occurs less frequently than GALANTHUS
NIVALIS and is distinguished from it by having
bigger flowers and broader glaucous leaves. It
also grows taller and prefers a sunny spot in the
garden.
Flower color and flowering period: white;
February-March.
Average plant height: 6-8 inches (15-20 cm).
Planting depth to base of bulb: 5 inches (12.5 cm)
Spacing between bulbs: 2 inches (5 cm).
Other characteristics are similar to G. NIVA-
LIS.

GALANTHUS NIVALIS

Common Snowdrop
Grows in the wild in woods and by streams.
Flower color and flowering period: white;
February-March.
Average plant height: 4 inches (10 cm).
Planting depth to base of bulb: 5 inches (12.5 cm)
Spacing between bulbs: 2 inches (5 cm).
Light requirements: Full to partial shade.
Landscape uses: borders, rock gardens, under
trees and shrubs, and in lawns. Species has
small bell-shaped, white flowers with green
spots. It has narrow glaucous leaves that are flat
in the sheath. It prefers a fertile and moist soil
and will grow in full sun to partial shade.
Perennializes in climatic zones 4 to 7 to form
beautiful groups.
There is one variety with double flowers:
GALANTHUS NIVALIS "Flore Pleno".

GALANTHUS ELWESII (Large-flowering snowdrops)

Geranium tuberosum

Family: Geraniaceae

A genus with more than 100 species, but only a few are bulbous. It should not be confused with GERANIUM PELARGONIUM, the commonly used garden geranium. GERANIUM TUBEROSUM is not extensively used.

Flower color and flowering period: rose; May.
Average plant height: 12 inches (30 cm).
Planting depth to base of bulb: 5 inches (12.5 cm)
Spacing between bulbs: 2 inches (5 cm).
Light requirements: Full sun.
Landscape uses: rock gardens and borders.

Numerous elegant flowers on supple stems with small, divided foliage (see photograph below). If they survive the first year, the bulbs are hardy and will perennialize.

GERANIUM TUBEROSUM.

GALANTHUS NIVALIS PLENUS "FLORE PLENO" (Double flowering snowdrop)

GLADIOLUS COLVILLI mixed

GLADIOLUS BYSANTINUS

GLADIOLUS COLVILLI "CHARM"

Gladiolus nanus

Family: Iridaceae

The name GLADIOLUS is derived from Latin Gladius meaning sword, and it refers to the shape of the leaves. The two species described, though flowering from the end of spring till early summer, should be planted in the fall and can be kept in the ground throughout the year. This is quite different from the other GLADIO-LUS species which must be planted in spring. Compared with the large flower types and the dwarf Gladiolus Butterfly, all of which flowering in late summer and early autumn, GLADIOLUS NANUS is not widely cultivated. It should not be confused with Gladiolus Butterfly.

Principal species

GLADIOLUS BYZANTINUS

Flower color and flowering period: violet-red; May-June.
Average plant height: 16-20 inches (40-50 cm).
Planting depth to base of bulb: 3 inches (7.5 cm).
Spacing between bulbs: 4 inches (10 cm).
Light requirements: Full sun.
Landscape uses: borders, rock gardens, and cut flowers.
GLADIOLUS prefers a sunny, well-drained soil, but also it grows well under less favorable conditions. In a heavy soil, the depth of planting should be reduced to 2 inches (5 cm). The violet-red flowers are spaced on long spikes growing on the upper half of the stem. This species is particularly adapted for use in rock gardens.

GLADIOLUS COLVILLI

A hybrid raised by W. Colvill a horticulturalist from Chelsea, England. It can be planted in the fall or in the spring.
Fall planting: The bulbs can be planted in pots which must be put on a place where they are protected from severe cold or in the full ground in a protected place covered with a layer of mulch.
Spring planting: Plant in March - May. Flowering will be in June-August.
Average plant height: 16-24 inches (40-60 cm).
Planting depth to base of bulb: 3 inches (7.5 cm).
Spacing between bulbs: 4 inches (10 cm).
Light requirements: Full sun.
Landscape uses: borders, rock gardens, and cut flowers.
The flowers, though small, are quite similar to those of the large flowering GLADIOLUS species. They have bright and varied colors and often have different colored spots.
The best-known cultivars of Nanus and other types are:
CHARM: salmon pink
FLORIADE: red and orange
FIANCEE: pure white
NYMPH: white and red
PEACH BLOSSOM: tender pink
QUEEN WILHELMINA: white and pink
SPITFIRE: bright red
WARMUNDA (Charming Beauty): pink and white.
All of them are very suitable for use as cut flowers.

Hyacinthus

Hyacinthus

Common name: DUTCH HYACINTHS
Family: Liliaceae

HYACINTHUS is derived from Hyakinthos, the name of a Greek hero killed by Apollo. Together with CROCUS, TULIPS and NARCISSUS (Daffodils), HYACINTHS are one of most important of the spring-flowering bulbs. This is due to a large number of cultivars that are available and their ease of growing. The Hyacinth is native to regions of the Mediterranean. For centuries its cultivation in Holland has been so important that the original name of HYACINTHUS ORIENTALIS is not well known, but Dutch Hyacinths are known world-wide. Its cultivation can be traced back to Greek and Roman times. In the 17th and 18th centuries, and especially in Holland, the speculation in flowering bulbs was such that a single bulb could cost $ 300 or more.

The cultivation of hyacinths is very easy and there are many uses for it. It is one of the most interesting flowers for interior decoration in winter (see chapter on forcing). The flowers have a pleasant smell.

BLUE MAGIC

Planting and cultivation

Flower color and flowering period:
red, pink, orange, salmon, yellow, purple and blue; March-April.

Average plant height: 8-10 inches (20-35 cm).

Planting depth to base of bulb: 6 inches (15 cm).

Spacing between bulbs: 3-4 inches (7.5-10 cm)

Light requirements: Full sun to partial shade.

Landscape uses: beds and borders.

Hyacinths prefer a fertile, well-drained soil. With heavy soils, drainage must be improved. Flowering can be prolonged by using a partial shade area. In contrast to other bulb species, the size of the hyacinth bulbs determines the bigness of the flowers. Big bulbs will produce bigger and more compact inflorescences. A discreet support of the stems e.g. a thin wire through the flower stalks, can be used to prevent them from bending and breaking. If the bulbs are planted in the garden, 15-16 and 16-17 cm bulbs should be used. Bigger bulbs are best suited for forcing. The bulbs can be left in the ground for 2 or 3 years, but the floral stem must be cut off after flowering. The leaves, however, should be left until they have completely senescenced.

Principal cultivars

About 100 varieties are cultivated, but almost 25 of them represent 90% of the total world production.

Hyacinths are often used in small groups of 3 to 5 bulbs of one cultivar or are planted in larger groups or beds with solid or mixed colors.

Deep blue
BLUE JACKET deep blue
BLUE MAGIC very deep violet-blue, white heart
DELFT BLUE blue
KING OF THE BLUES deep blue
OSTARA deep violet-blue

Light blue
BLUE GIANT luminous blue
PERLE BRILLANTE Luminous bright blue

Mauve-violet
AMETHYST lilac-blue
VIOLET PEARL purple violet

Red
AMSTERDAM deep carmine red
HOLLYHOCK deep red, double flowers
JAN BOS carmine-red

Pink
ANNA MARIE bright pink
LADY DERBY salmon pink
MARCONI deep pink
PINK PEARL brilliant bright pink
QUEEN OF THE PINKS bright pink

Yellow
CITY OF HAARLEM bright yellow

Orange
GIPSY QUEEN salmon orange
ORANJE BOVEN salmon orange

White
CARNEGIE pure white
L'INNOCENCE pure white
WHITE PEARL pure white

Amongst the above-mentioned cultivars some truly excel in the beauty of their flower colors.
BLUE MAGIC very deep blue, semi-double flowers with white hearts; a recent cultivar.
HOLLYHOCK deep red with double flowers, a recent variety
AMETHYST luminous purple mauve
GIPSY QUEEN small but very elegant, salmon orange flowers; a very special, recent variety.
CARNEGIE perfect pure white.

JAN BOS   KING OF THE BLUES

QUEEN OF THE PINKS

CARNEGIE

HOLLYHOCK, double flowers

CITY OF HAARLEM

PERLE BRILLANTE

AMETHYST

GIPSY QUEEN

DELFT BLUE

LADY
DERBY ▶

ANNA MARIE

OSTARA

65

Other Hyacinthus species

HYACINTHUS MULTIFLORA

This is not a species, but hyacinth bulbs that have undergone a handling procedure. The basal plate has been removed so that small bulbs develop. Planted in pots or in the garden they produce small compact racemes of flowers (see photograph on right). They are less spectacular than the normal cultivars with big flowers. Thus, they are used as a special interest item.

HYACINTHUS AMETHYSTINUS

synonym: BRIMEURA AMETHYSTINA
Hyacinth of Spain or the Pyrenees. This species is not widely grown.
Flower color and flowering period: pale blue or white; May-June.
Average plant height: 8 inches (20 cm).
Planting depth to base of bulb: 5 inches (12.5 cm)
Spacing between bulbs: 2 inches (5 cm).
Landscape uses: beds and borders.

HYACINTHUS AZUREUS

synonym: HYACINTHELLA AZUREA
MUSCARI AZUREUM (see page 76 for details on this species).

HYACINTHUS ORIENTALIS ALBULUS

Species is not widely used.
synonym: BELLEVALIA ROMANA
Roman Hyacinth.
Flower color and flowering period: blue, pink and white; March.
Average plant height: 10-12 inches (25-30 cm).

HYACINTHUS ORIENTALIS ALBULUS
The original multi-flowered hyacinth.

Ipheion uniflorum

Family: Liliaceae
synonyms: TRITELEIA UNIFLORA
Common name: TRITELEIA UNIFLORUM.

Flower color and flowering period: white, blue violet; April-May.
Average plant height: 5 inches (12.5 cm).
Planting depth to base of bulb: 5 inches (12.5 cm)
Spacing between bulbs: 2 inches (5 cm).
Light requirements: Full sun.
Landscape uses: borders and rock gardens.

This genus has about twenty species that are native to South America. However, only one species is cultivated and on a small scale. Although it is hardy, IPHEION should be planted in a sheltered place in climatic zones 5 and 6. Like many other bulbs, IPHEION requires a well-drained soil. The bulbs should be left in the soil to perennialize and to form beautiful clumps of flowers. The flowers are star-shaped, solitary and have a soapy odor (see photograph on right). The grass-like leaves, when crushed, have a faint onion smell.

Principal cultivars
VIOLACEUM: white with blue midrib
WISLEY BLUE: deep violet-blue

IPHEION UNIFLORUM

Dutch Iris

Iris

Family: Iridaceae

This genus is highly complicated and consists of numerous sections with more than 200 different species. In this book only, the bulbous species are described. The species with rhizomes are considered to be perennial plants and they are very popular, especially IRIS GERMANICA. The bulbous species are excellent for the garden and most can be used as cut flowers.

Principal species

IRIS ANGLICA
English Iris
synonym: IRIS LATIFOLIA
Common name: ENGLISH IRIS
Flower color and flowering period: white, purple and blue; June-July.
Average plant height: 20 inches (50 cm).
Planting depth to base of bulb: 8 inches (20 cm).
Spacing between bulbs: 4 inches (10 cm).
Light requirements: Full sun.
Landscape uses: beds, borders, and cut flowers.
This species is cultivated in the same way as IRIS HOLLANDICA (Dutch Iris), which is a well known species. The bulbs prefer to be kept in the soil. The foliage appears in early spring. Two or three, 4-5 inches (10-12.5 cm), flowers are borne on strong stems. There is an assortment of white, blue and violet hybrids grown commercially.

IRIS BUCHARICA
Flower color and flowering period: white and golden-yellow; April-May.
Average plant height: 16 inches (40 cm).
Planting depth to base of bulb: 5 inches (12.5 cm).
Spacing between bulbs: 4 inches (10 cm).
Light requirements: Full sun.
Landscape uses: beds, borders, and cut flowers.
This species is native to Central Asia. Each stem has two colored, 3 inches (7.5 cm) fragrant flowers. It is not well known, but is easy to cultivate like Dutch Iris.

IRIS DANFORDIAE
Flower color and flowering period: bright yellow; February-April.
Average plant height: 4 inches (10 cm).
Planting depth to base of bulb: 5 inches (12.5 cm)
Spacing between bulbs: 1 inch (2.5 cm).
Light requirements: Full sun to partial shade.
Landscape uses: borders, rock gardens, and under shrubs and trees.
Species is native to Turkey. The flowers have little brown spots.

IRIS BUCHARICA   IRIS DANFORDIAE

IRIS HISTRIOIDES "MAJOR"

DUTCH IRIS 'BRONZE QUEEN'

DUTCH IRIS
'BLUE RIBBON'

IRIS HISTRIOIDES "Major"

Flower color and flowering period: blue;
February-March.
Average plant height: 3 inches (7.5 cm).
Planting depth to base of bulb: 5 inches (12.5 cm)
Spacing between bulbs: 2 inches (5 cm).
Light requirements: Full sun to partial shade.
Landscape uses: rock gardens and under trees
and shrubs.

Native to Central Turkey, it is one of the most
beautiful species of dwarf Iris. However, it is not
widely used. The big flowers are deep blue with
orange and white spots on upper sides of petals.

DUTCH IRIS

Flower color and flowering period: deep and
light blue, purple, yellow and white: May-June.
Average plant height: 20 inches (20 cm).
Planting depth to base of bulb: 5 inches (12.5 cm)
Spacing between bulbs: 4 inches (10 cm).
Light requirements: Full sun.
Landscape uses: beds, borders, and cut flowers.

This is a hybrid that was initially produced by
the Dutch grower Van Tubergen by cross-breeding of three wild Iris species. Commercially,
many cultivars are grown on a large scale for use
as cut flowers. It prefers a fertile, sandy and
well-drained soil. This species is best suited for
climatic zones 8 and 9. Bulbs can be left in the
ground, but leaves should not be cut off until
they are completely dried. The 4 inch (10 cm)
flowers are borne on strong stems. If seed pods
are formed they should be removed to promote
growth of the daughter bulbs.

There are a great number of cultivars with rich
colors. The most available ones are:
APOLLO: yellow and white
BLUE MAGIC: deep purple-blue
BLUE RIBBON: deep blue
BRONZE QUEEN: bronze and yellow
FRANS HALS: light lavender
GOLDEN HARVEST: golden yellow
H.C. VAN VLIET: medium-blue
HILDEGARDE: light blue
IDEAL: sky blue
IMPERATOR: blue and orange
MARQUETTE: cream-white, yellow and
orange
PURPLE SENSATION: deep purple
SYMPHONY: yellow and white
TELSTAR: deep blue
WEDGWOOD: blue and yellow
WHITE EXCELSIOR: pure white
WHITE PERFECTION: pure white
WHITE VAN VLIET: pure white
WHITE WEDGWOOD: pure white
The cultivars are also offered for sale in mixed
assortments.

DUTCH IRIS 'FRANS HALS'   DUTCH IRIS 'GOLDEN HARVEST'   IRIS RETICULATA 'JOYCE'

IRIS RETICULATA

Flower color and flowering period: purple, light and dark blue; February-April.
Average plant height: 5 inches (12.5 cm).
Planting depth to base of bulb: 5 inches (12.5 cm)
Spacing between bulbs: 2 inches (5 cm).
Light requirements: Full sun to partial shade.
Landscape uses: borders, rock gardens, and under trees and shrubs.

Native to the Caucasus and Iran, IRIS RETICULATA are widely cultivated. It is one of the best species for spring rock gardens. It grows in any well-drained soil and the bulbs should be left in the soil after flowering. They tend to perennialize in climatic zones 4 to 8. The sweet-scented flowers are spotted yellow.

The most available varieties are:
CANTAB: light blue
HARMONY: blue
JOYCE: deep violet blue
J.S. DIJT: purple-violet
VIOLET BEAUTY: Purple violet

IRIS TUBEROSA

synonym: HERMODACTYLUS TUBEROSUS
Common names: Snake's Head Iris, Widow Iris.
Flower color and flowering period: greenish with falls being purple brown; April.
Average plant height: 8 inches (20 cm).
Planting depth to base of bulb: 5 inches (12.5 cm)
Spacing between bulbs: 4 inches (10 cm).
Light requirements: Full sun to partial shade.
Landscape uses: rock gardens.

This species is native to the Mediterranean regions of Europe. It is one of the rarest and most unusual species. Hence, its English name of Snake's Head Iris.

DUTCH IRIS 'H.C. VAN VLIET'   DUTCH IRIS 'PURPLE SENSATION'

IRIS RETICULATA "VIOLET BEAUTY"   IRIS RETICULATA "J.S. DIJT"

IRIS RETICULATA "HARMONY"   IRIS TUBEROSA

Ixiolirion pallasii

Synonym: IXIOLIRION MONTANUM,
IXIOLIRION TATARICUM
Family: Amaryllidaceae

Flower color and flowering period: light purple;
May-June.
Average plant height: 10-14 inches (20-35 cm).
Planting depth to base of bulb: 5 inches (12.5 cm).
Spacing between bulbs: 2 inches (5 cm).
Light requirements: Full sun.
Landscape uses: borders, rock gardens, and cut
flowers.

This genus is native to the steppes of Central
Asia and has relatively few species. The star-
shaped, violet-blue, elegant flowers highly suitable as cut flowers (see photograph on page
73). It prefers a fertile, well-drained soil. The
bulbs are hardy and tend to perennialize in climatic zones 4 to 7.

Ixia hybrids

Family: Iridaceae

The bulbs cultivated under the name IXIA are
mostly hybrids. The original two species, IXIA
PANICULATA with cream-colored flowers
and brown hearts and IXIA VIRIDIFLORA
with green-blue flowers, are seldom cultivated
and come from South Africa. The hybrids have
several elegant flowers borne on straw-like
stems.
Flower color and flowering period: white, yellow, orange, pink, and red; March-June.
Average plant height: 16 inches (40 cm).
Planting depth to base of bulb: 5 inches (12.5 cm)
Spacing between bulbs: 3 inches (7.5 cm).
Light requirements: Full sun.
Landscape uses: beds, borders, and cut flowers.

Cultivation outside

The bulbs are not hardy. They grow and flower
best in regions with mild winters (climatic
zones 7-9). They should be planted in sheltered
areas and covered with a mulch for the winter.
They should not be planted too early, the best
period being October to November. This helps
to avoid precocious leaf growth and subsequent
damage by frost. IXIA prefers a sandy, well-
drained soil. Ixias do not tend to perennialize
easily.

Lachenalia tricolor

Synonym: LACHENALIA ALOIDES
Family: Liliaceae

Flower color and flowering period: yellow,
orange, green and red; December-March.
Average plant height: 9 inches (25 cm).
Planting depth to base of bulb: 5 inches (12.5 cm)
Spacing between bulbs: 2 inches (5 cm).
Light requirements: Full sun.
Landscape uses: indoor cultivation in pots.

The bell-shaped 3 colored flowers (see photograph on page 73), are borne on 10-12 inches (25-
30 cm) long stems. It has fragile, supple and
bending, deep green leaves with purple-brown
spots. The genus is native to South Africa and
consists of about 50 species. However, only
LACHENALIA TRICOLOR is cultivated
commercially.
The bulbs are not hardy. Therefore, the best
results can be obtained only when the bulbs are
cultivated indoors. Even in areas with very mild
temperatures throughout the year the bulbs
require a well-sheltered position when planted
in the garden.

Cultivation in pots

Plant 5-7 bulbs in a 6 inch (15 cm) diameter pot.
This should be done in mid-October. Use a
well-drained potting mix. Then place the pot in
a well lighted room that will not freeze. As soon
as the floral stems appear the pot can be placed
in the home. The length of the flowering period
is longest if the temperature in the home is kept
as low as possible. After flowering, reduce the
amount of water given to the plants. When the
leaves have senescenced, the pot must be placed in a dry place for a rest period. The bulbs
multiply easily sand they should be divided in
the fall. There are some varieties of LACHE-
NALIA TRICOLOR available, but all of them
have yellow, green, orange and red flowers.

IXIOLIRION PALLASII

LACHENALIA TRICOLOR

Leucojum

Family: Amaryllidaceae

This genus consists of a dozen species and is very often confused with GALANTHUS (Snowdrops). This is understandable since they have some similar characteristics. LEUCOJUM also resembles Lily-of-the-Valley (CONVALLARIA) except for its height and bigger flowers.

Principal species

Only two species are cultivated and their use in the garden is very easy. These bulbs should be used more extensively than they are currently used.

LEUCOJUM AESTIVUM

Summer Snowflake.
Even though it has the name AESTIVUM (of the summer), this species flowers in April-May.
Flower color and flowering period: white; April-May.
Average plant height: 14-24 inches (35-60 cm).
Planting depth to base of bulb: 5 inches (12.5 cm)
Spacing between bulbs: 3 inches (7.5 cm).
Light requirements: Full sun to partial shade.
Landscape uses: borders, rock gardens, under shrubs and trees, and as cut flowers.
Normally there are 3-5 bell-shaped, green-edged flowers on a stem. The leaves are bright green along and narrow.
The cultivar, 'Gravetye Giant', is very vigorous and can reach a height of 24 inches (60 cm).

LEUCOJUM VERNUM

Spring Snowflake.
Flower color and flowering period: white; February-March.
Average plant height: 8 inches (20 cm).
Planting depth to base of bulb: 5 inches (12.5 cm)
Spacing between bulbs: 3 inches (7.5 cm).
Light requirements: Full sun to partial shade.
Landscape uses: borders, rock gardens, and under shrubs and trees.
Species flowers very early in the spring, just as soon as the snow melts. The white bell-shaped flowers have a green spot on each petal. Usually there are 5 flowers on a stem. The foliage is bright green, long and narrow.

Planting and cultivation

Both species are cultivated identically. They should be planted in September-October and grow best in a well-drained soil. The bulbs prefer to be kept in the ground where they grow and perennialize easily. If the bulbs become very compact, they must be divided, because the excessive foliage is detrimental to the development of the flowers. They will tolerate slightly moist conditions and, thus, can be grown along brooks and ponds.

LEUCOJUM VERNUM

73

Lilium candidum

Common names: MADONNA LILY
Family: Liliaceae

This species is native to Asia-Minor and is a well known lily species. It has been cultivated for centuries and has not changed greatly over time. Contrary to what is believed by some, this lily is not the origin of the famous 'fleur-de-lis' emblem of the French monarchy.

This lily must be planted in early fall. The bulbs are marketed at the same time as the other spring-flowering bulbs. It should be noted that the Madonna Lily is difficult to grow in the U.S. All other lily species flower in June-August and can be planted either in fall or in spring. These lilies will be described in another book on summer-flowering bulbs.

Planting and cultivation

Flower color and flowering period: pure white; June-July.

Average plant height: 24-40 inches (60-100 cm).

Special planting instructions: Bulbs must be planted so that only 1 inch of soil covers the nose of the bulb.

Spacing between bulbs: 8 inches (20 cm).

Light requirements: Full sun.

Landscape uses: borders, beds with perennial plants, and cut flowers.

Species grows in any soil, but prefers a fertile, well-drained pH 7.0 soil. The foliage disappears after flowering. Young shoots will then develop and the new leaves persistent through winter. That is why the bulbs are best planted in August-September. Once planted, the bulbs should not be moved.

The magnificent, big, white flowers have golden-yellow hearts and stamens (see photograph on right). As with all lilies, the lowest flowers open first. The sweet-smelling flowers are used to make perfumes and scents and have long been considered as an excellent medicinal plant. It is an excellent cut flower.

MADONNA LILY

Muscari

Family: Liliaceae

This genus consists of about 60 species that are native to Europe and Asia-Minor. At present, six of them are widely cultivated and the best-known is MUSCARI ARMENIACUM (Grape hyacinth). All are hardy, grow well in any well-drained soil. They are extremely easy to culti-vate. A must for every garden.

Planting and cultivation

Flower color and flowering period: blue, purple or white; March-May, depending on the species.

Average plant height: 4-8 inches (10-20 cm).
Planting depth to base of bulb: 5 inches (12.5 cm)
Spacing between bulbs: 1 inch (2.5 cm) to 3 inches (7.5 cm), depending on the species.
Light requirements: Full sun to partial shade.
Landscape uses: borders, rock gardens, and under shrubs and trees.

Muscaris do not require a special soil or location, but an excess of water will damage them. They prefer to be left in the soil, where they perennialize (climatic zones 4-8). If they become too thick, they can be divided. This plant and especially MUSCARI ARMENIA-CUM is excellent for parks, fields, and large flo-wer-beds.

The famous long "blue river" between decora-tive shrubs in the Keukenhof Garden in Lisse, The Netherlands, in one of the most admired and photographed spots of this spectacular park. Muscaris are also excellent for cultiva-tion in pots. (See Chapter on Forcing).

Principal species

MUSCARI ARMENIACUM

Common name: GRAPE HYACINTH.

This is the best-known species and has intense blue flowers, white-lined at the edges, in com-pact bunches on strong stems. The flowers last a long time and it usually flowers in April-May. The species naturalizes quickly and when it does, the long leaves usually develop in the fall and then over winter.

Principal varieties
CANTAB: less intense blue than the normal flower type.
HEAVENLY BLUE: very intense blue.
BLUE SPIKE: cultivar has double flowers and is lighter blue than the other.

MUSCARI ARMENIACUM "CANTAB"   MUSCARI ARMENIACUM "BLUE SPIKE"

MUSCARI COMOSUM PLUMOSUM

MUSCARI AZUREUM

synonym: HYACINTHELLA AZUREA
Commercially, this species is sold as a grape hyacinth even though it is not a MUSCARI. It is native to Asia-Minor. Flowers are in compact bunches. It has luminous bright blue-green leaves that are shorter than other species. The bulbs are hardy and should be planted very close together to get the maximum effect in the garden (see photograph above). It tends to perennialize in climatic zones 4-8.

MUSCARI BOTRYOIDES ALBUM

Species is very close to MUSCARI ARMENIACUM. It has narrow and less compact bunches on white flowers. There is a blue variety, but it is rarely cultivated. The species perennializes in climatic zones 4-8. The bulbs should be planted very close together to get the maximum effect in the garden (see photograph above).

MUSCARI COMOSUM "PLUMOSUM"

Common name: FEATHER HYACINTH.
This species differs from the other species by its height and shape of the flowers. It has mauve-lilac, double, plume-like flowers on 6 inch (15 cm) long stems in May-June. They are very decorative in small groups, with the bulbs planted about 4 inches (10 cm) apart (see photograph above). This species does not tend to perennialize easily.

MUSCARI LATIFOLIUM

Species is not extensively cultivated. Small blue-purple flowers are on compact inflorescence, on 10-12 inches (25-30 cm) stems. Flowers in April-May. An excellent plant for rock gardens.

MUSCARI TUBERGENIANUM

One of the numerous plants raised by the Dutch bulb grower Van Tubergen. It is native to Persia and a rather recent introduction. It deserves to become better-known and more widely used. It flowers in March-April and has compact bunches of light and deep blue flowers on 8 inches (20 cm) stems. It is easy to grow and is very beautiful in rock gardens.

MUSCARI LATIFOLIUM.

Narcissus

Narcissus

Common names: DAFFODILS, JONQUILS
Family: Amaryllidaceae

Together with CROCUS, HYACINTHS and TULIPS, the NARCISSUS are one of the most important and popular spring flowering bulbs. NARCISSUS are widely cultivated due to the range of hardiness of the bulbs, the many uses, colors, flower types, and their easy cultivation. The English strongly compete with the Dutch in the amount of bulb production and they lead the world in the development of new cultivars. The Royal Horticultural Society in London is the most authoritative institution for NARCISSUS.

The intense culture of NARCISSUS began about 1500 A.D., but references to them can be found as early as 300 B.C. The principal colors are white, yellow, red, orange and salmon-pink. Shape and size of flowers, height of stems and periods of flowering differ according to the species and cultivars. The narrow, ribbon-like foliage is either completely green or it is bluish-green. As with Tulips, the horticultural and botanic species are classified separately. Commercially, there are over 300 cultivars available.

The major parents of the horticultural cultivars are NARCISSUS POETICUS (of the poets) and NARCISSUS PSEUDONARCISSUS (Jonquil-Daffodil). There are a great many wild species and they are difficult to classify.

Nearly all species have a distinct and pleasant smell. That is why the flowers are very important for the production of perfumes and scents. All species are native to Europe and, therefore, most of them are hardy. The exceptions are some cultivars of NARCISSUS TAZETTA, that are native to Asia and Africa and these are hardy in only regions with a mild climate (climatic zones 9 and 10).

Classification

To understand fully certain definitions and the categories of species and varieties it is necessary to know the different parts of the NARCISSUS (see photograph below). The six petals are known as the perianth and the center is known as a trumpet, cup or corona depending on its size and shape. To simplify the botanical classification of this important genus, the species and subspecies are divided into the following divisions.

Division 1:
TRUMPET DAFFODILS OF GARDEN ORIGIN
Distinguishing characters: One flower to a stem; trumpet or corona as long or longer than the perianth segments.

Division 2:
LARGE-CUPPED DAFFODILS OF GARDEN ORIGIN
Distinguishing characters: One flower to a stem; cup or corona more than one-third, but less than equal to the length of the perianth segments.

Division 3:
SMALL-CUPPED DAFFODILS OF GARDEN ORIGIN
Distinguishing characters: One flower to a stem; cup or corona not more than one-third the length of the perianth segments.

Division 4:
DOUBLE DAFFODILS OF GARDEN ORIGIN
Distinguishing characters: Double flowers.

Division 5:
TRIANDRUS DAFFODILS OF GARDEN ORIGIN
Distinguishing characters: Characteristics of NARCISSUS TRIANDRUS Predominant.

Division 6:
CYCLAMINEUS DAFFODILS OF GARDEN ORIGIN
Distinguishing characters: Characteristics of NARCISSUS CYCLAMINEUS predominant.

Division 7:
JONQUILLA DAFFODILS OF GARDEN ORIGIN
Distinguishing characters: Characteristics of the NARCISSUS JONQUILLA group. predominant.

Division 8:
TAZETTA DAFFODILS OF GARDEN ORIGIN
Distinguishing characters: Characteristics of the NARCISSUS TAZETTA group predominant.

Division 9:
POETICUS DAFFODILS OF GARDEN ORIGIN
Distinguishing characters: Characteristics of the NARCISSUS POETICUS group predominant.

Division 10:
SPECIES AND WILD FORMS AND WILD HYBRIDS
All species and wild or reputedly wild forms and hybrids. Double forms of these varieties are included.

Division 11:
SPLIT-CORONA DAFFODILS OF GARDEN ORIGIN
Distinguishing characters: Corona split for at least one-third of its length.

Division 12:
MISCELLANEOUS DAFFODILS
All daffodils not falling into any one of the foregoing Divisions.
For practical reasons, very close species or types have been grouped together.

Planting and cultivation

With the exception of some of N. TAZETTA and certain species, most NARCISSUS are hardy. Bulbs properly planted in the fall will survive even the severest winters. They can be left in the ground for many years where they multiply very quickly to form beautiful and compact groups. Flowering is almost always more beautiful in the second and third season. Should you wish to divide the bulb groups, harvest them immediately after the foliage has died. Then replant as soon as possible or store at 63°-68°F (17-20°C) until they are planted. When out of the ground, they must be stored in well ventilated trays and areas.

The TAZETTA varieties (paperwhites) which can only be planted outside in climatic zones 9 and 10 are particularly suited for cultivation indoors for flowering around Christmas (see Chapter on Forcing).

NARCISSUS grow best in a well-drained pH 6-7 soil.

NARCISSUS does not require a special location in the garden. They grow well in the full shade, partial shade and full sun. Thus, they can be used in almost any part of the landscape.

Flower color and flowering period: white, yellow, orange, red and pink; February-May.

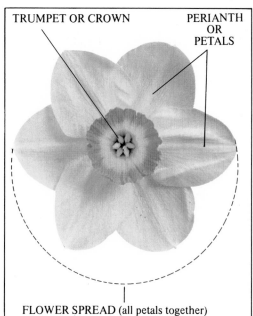

TRUMPET OR CROWN

PERIANTH OR PETALS

FLOWER SPREAD (all petals together)

NARCISSUS FLOWER and its parts

TRUMPET   LARGE CUP   SMALL CUP

The difference between three important types of Narcissus:
The photo clearly shows the difference in the size of the trumpet or crown, also called cup.

MAGNET

SPELLBINDER

Average plant height: 4-16 inches (10-40 cm).
Planting depth to base of bulb: Large bulbs, 8 inches (20 cm); small bulbs, 5 inches (12.5 cm).
Spacing between bulbs: 3 inches (7.5 cm) for large bulbs; 1 inch (2.5 cm) for small bulbs).
Light requirements: Full sun to full shade.
Landscape uses: NARCISSUS are suited to almost all possible applications: fields, beds, borders, rock gardens, cut flowers and forcing. When using daffodils as cut flowers, there is one word of caution: do not place fresh cut flowers in the same water with fresh cut tulips. One should first place the NARCISSUS flowers in its own water overnight, then combine them with tulips. It is also possible to first dip the cut NARCISSUS in a dilute solution of bleach and then combine the flowers. The principal species are described and illustrated and their best-known cultivars are mentioned. NARCISSUS can be purchased either by cultivar or in mixed assortments.

Principal species

NARCISSUS TRUMPET

One of the most widely cultivated types. The trumpet is equal to or longer than the segments of the perianth.
Flower color and flowering period: yellow, white, and bicolored; March-May.
Average plant height: 16-20 inches (35-50 cm).
Spacing between bulbs: 2-3 inches (5-7.5 cm).
The big flowers can bend the stems and accentuate the forward inclination that is characteristic of most species of NARCISSUS.
Principal cultivars
BALLADE: golden-yellow
BEERSHEBA: white
BRIGHTON: golden-yellow with lemon-yellow trumpet
DUTCH MASTER*: golden-yellow
EXPLORER*: golden-yellow
FORESIGHT: white, bright yellow trumpet
GOBLET*: creamy-white, yellow trumpet
GOLDEN HARVEST*: gold-yellow
GOLD MEDAL*: gold-yellow

*Cultivars recommended for forcing.

GOLDEN HARVEST

PINK BEAUTY

KING ALFRED

QUEEN OF BICOLORS

MOUNT HOOD

UNSURPASSABLE

GIGANTIC STAR

BEERSHEBA.

ROYAL GOLD

81

NARCISSUS TRUMPET
(continuation)

KING ALFRED: canary-yellow
MAGNET*: white, yellow trumpet
MOUNT HOOD*: ivory-white
PINK BEAUTY: white-salmon-pink trumpet
QUEEN OF BICOLORS: white, yellow trumpet
REMBRANDT: canary yellow
ROYAL GOLD: yellow
SPELLBINDER: canary yellow, pale yellow trumpet
UNSURPASSABLE*: canary yellow, gold-yellow trumpet

SALOME

LARGE-CUPPED NARCISSUS

The trumpet of this group is called a cup. Its length is smaller than a segment of the perianth, but never smaller than one third. All cultivars have one flower to a stem.

Flower color and flowering period: yellow, white and bicolored; March-May.

Average plant height: 12-20 inches (30-50 cm).

Spacing between bulbs: 2-3 inches (5-7.5 cm).

Flowers are equally large as the trumpet NARCISSUS, but the cup is smaller. The range of colors is larger and it is a most important division with a large number of cultivars.

Principal cultivars

AMOR: white, cup golden - yellow and orange
ARMADA: yellow, with orange cup
CARLTON*: Canary-yellow, gold-yellow cup
DELIBES: creamy yellow, orange cup
DUKE OF WINDSOR: white, yellow cup
FLOWER RECORD*: white, yellow and red cup
FORTUNE*: canary-yellow, orange cup
GIGANTIC STAR: canary-yellow
ICE FOLLIES*: white, canary-yellow cup
JUANITA: canary-yellow, bright orange cup
PROFESSOR EINSTEIN: white, bright orange cup
QUIRINUS: yellow with red cup
SALOME: white, salmon-colored cup
SATIN PINK: white, salmon-colored cup
SCARLET ELEGANCE: yellow, vermillion and orange cup
SCARLET O'HARA: bright yellow, luminous orange cup
SUN CHARIOT: yellow with orange cup
YELLOW SUN*: canary-yellow, yellow cup

* Cultivars recommended for forcing.

82

DUKE OF WINDSOR

ARMADA

ICE FOLLIES

SUN CHARIOT

LARGE-CUPPED NARCISSUS

FLOWER RECORD

SMALL-CUPPED NARCISSUS
The cup is smaller than that of the large-cupped division; it is less than one third of a segment of the perianth. All cultivars have one flower to a stem.

Flower color and flowering period: white, yellow and bicolored; March-May.

Average plant height: 10-20 inches (25-50 cm).
Spacing between bulbs: 2-3 inches (5-7.5 cm).

The flowers are as big as those of the two preceeding divisions, but the cup is shorter. This division has the same range of attractive colors as the 2 previous divisions.

Principal cultivars
AFLAME: white, orange and yellow cup
BARRETT BROWNING*: white, bright orange cup
BIRMA: clear yellow, orange cup
EDWARD BUXTON: yellow, red cup
POMONA: white, red cup
SCARLET ROYAL: yellow, orange cup
VERGER: white, orange and yellow cup

* Cultivars recommended for forcing.

PROFESSOR EINSTEIN

QUIRINUS

SCARLET ROYAL

EDWARD BUXTON

BARRETT BROWNING

POMONA

NARCISSUS WITH DOUBLE FLOWERS

The flowers have a perianth size similar to the previous divisions, however, the double flowers do not form a distinct cup. They give a somewhat rumpled effect (see photographs on page 86).

Flower color and flowering period: yellow, white, and red; April-May.

Average plant height: 12-16 inches (30-40 cm).

Spacing between bulbs: 2-3 inches (5-7.5 cm).

The cultivars of this division have one flower to a stem. Because of their large flower head, they do not do well under heavy rains. Also, they do not do well in very hot climates (climatic zones 8-10).

If they are to be used as cut flowers, do not cut before the flower is fully open.

Principal cultivars

DICK WILDEN: perianth and cup golden-yellow

FLOWER DRIFT*: creamy white, white, yellow and orange cup

GOLDEN DUCAT: perianth and cup golden-yellow

INGLESCOMBE*: perianth and cup golden-yellow

MARY COPELAND: white, cup white and orange-red

TAHITI: gold-yellow, cup gold yellow and vermillion

TEXAS: lemon-yellow, cup yellow and orange

VAN SION*: perianth and cup lemon-yellow

WHITE LION: ivory-white, cup ivory and pale yellow

* Cultivars with smaller flowers and stems (25-30 cm).

TAHITI

INGLESCOMBE

WHITE LION

NARCISSUS SPLIT

A recent creation with unusual flowers. The perianth is similar to that of the large cupped NARCISSUS, but the cup is spread open in such a way that they resemble a butterfly.
Flower color and flowering period: yellow, white, and orange; April-May
Average plant height: 16-20 inches (40-50 cm).
Spacing between bulbs: 3 inches (7.5 cm).
Grows the same as large cupped NARCISSUS.
An interesting species for use as cut flowers.
There is one flower to a stem.

Principal varieties
BACCARAT: perianth and cup gold-yellow
CASSATA*: yellowish perianth, cup lemon-yellow
CHANTERELLE: creamy white perianth, cup lemon-yellow
ORANGERY: white perianth, bright orange cup
PARISIENNE: creamy white perianth, bright orange cup

* Cultivar recommended for forcing.

These cultivars are often sold in mixed assortments.

FLOWER DRIFT

VAN SION

Mixed SPLIT CORONA NARCISSUS

NARCISSUS TRIANDRUS "LIBERTY BELLS"

NARCISSUS TRIANDRUS
"THALIA"

NARCISSUS TRIANDRUS

The cultivars of this division have 2-6 flowers to a stem (multiflowered). Sizes of the cups differ according to cultivars. The petals of the perianth are often curved backwards.
Flower color and flowering period: white and yellow; March-April
Average plant height: 10-12 inches (25-30 cm)
Spacing between bulbs: 2 inches (5 cm)
Grows shorter and with less foliage than the previous divisions. They are particularly useful for rock gardens and prefer a moist soil. This species is less known and grown than previous ones.

Principal varieties
HAWERA: gold-yellow
LIBERTY BELLS: lemon-yellow
THALIA: pure white
TRESAMBLE: white

NARCISSUS CYCLAMINEUS

This dwarf species owes its name to fact that its flowers resemble those of cyclamen. The petals of the perianth almost completely curved backwards (see photographs on page 89). The flowers form a trumpet. They are often equally long as the segments of the perianth and they can have undulant fringes. The flowers slightly bend the tops of the stems.

Principal cultivars
BABY DOLL: gold-yellow, tube lemon-yellow
CHARITY MAY: gold-yellow
FEBRUARY GOLD: gold-yellow
FEBRUARY SILVER: white, yellow trumpet
JACK SNIPE: ivory-white, yellow trumpet
JUMBLIE*: gold-yellow
MARCH SUNSHINE: perianth bright yellow, trumpet deep yellow
PEEPING TOM: lemon-yellow
TETE A TETE*: lemon-yellow, very suitable for indoor-forcing
W.P. MILNER: creamy yellow with long trumpet

* multiflowered types.

The cultivars, February Gold, Jack Snipe, Peeping Tom and Tete a Tete can be forced.

NARCISSUS TRIANDRUS "HAWERA"

NARCISSUS CYCLAMINEUS "FEBRUARY SILVER" NARCISSUS CYCLAMINEUS "TETE A TETE"

NARCISSUS CYCLAMINEUS "W.P. MILNER"

NARCISSUS CYCLAMINEUS
"PEEPING TOM"

NARCISSUS CYCLAMINEUS "JACK SNIPE"

NARCISSUS JONQUIL

Narcissus Jonquilla
Also called Small Jonquil. It should not be confused with the real Jonquil, NARCISSUS PSEUDONARCISSUS. The yellow flowers form a crown smaller than half the segments of the perianth.

Flower color and flowering period: yellow, with yellow or orange cups; April-June.
Average plant height: 10-14 inches (25-35 cm).
Spacing between bulbs: 2-3 inches (5-7.5 cm).
The flowers are sweet-smelling and there are 2-6 to a stem. The cultivars of this division prefer a sunny position and are useful in fields, beds and as cut flowers.

Principal varieties
BABY MOON: gold-yellow
GOLDEN PERFECTION: gold-yellow
LINTIE: white, yellow cup with white edge
SUGARBUSH: canary-yellow, orange cup
SUZY: gold-yellow, cup bright orange
SWEETNESS: gold-yellow
SWEET PEPPER: canary yellow, orange cup
TREVITHIAN: lemon-yellow

NARCISSUS JONQUILLA
"TREVITHIAN"

NARCISSUS JONQUILLA
"SUZY"

NARCISSUS JONQUILLA "BABY MOON"

NARCISSUS TAZETTA "CRAGFORD"

NARCISSUS TAZETTA

The cultivars of the species NARCISSUS POE-
TAZ and NARCISSUS POLYANTHUS are
combined in this division. All of them are multiflowered, with 4-8 flowers per stem. The cup is
distinctly smaller than the perianth. Some cultivars have double flowers and all are very sweet-
smelling.

Flower color and flowering period: white and
yellow with white, yellow or orange centers;
March-April.

Average plant height: 6-14 inches (15-35 cm).

Spacing between bulbs: 2 inches (5 cm).

This division consists of very different types,
some of them are suited for indoor forcing. It
includes the famous Paperwhite NARCISSUS.
The cultivars recommended for indoor-cultiva-
tion* are not winterhardy and should be planted in the garden only in climatic zones 9 and 10.
The other cultivars are suitable for fields, beds,
and as cut flowers.

Principal cultivars

BRIDAL CROWN *: white with orange
CHEERFULNESS: white
CRAGFORD*: white perianth, vermillion-red
cup
GERANIUM: white perianth, orange cup
GRAND SOLEIL D'OR*: gold-yellow, orange
cup
MINNOW (1): lemon yellow, cup golden yellow
SCARLET GEM: pale yellow, orange cup
SILVER CHIMES (1): very pale yellow, deeper
yellow cup, late flowering
YELLOW CHEERFULNESS: yellow
TOTUS ALBUS* (PAPERWHITE): pure
white

* Cultivars recommended for forcing indoors.
(1) dwarf varieties with small flowers.

NARCISSUS TAZETTA DOUBLE "BRIDAL CROWN"   NARCISSUS TAZETTA "SCARLET GEM"

NARCISSUS TAZETTA "GERANIUM"

NARCISSUS POETICUS
(of the Poets)

This is not a division, but a species and practically is limited to one commercial cultivar. The big flowers have a white perianth and a short, flat cup.

Flower color and flowering period: white, yellow cup with an orange edge; April-May.

Average plant height: 12-16 inches (30-40 cm).

Spacing between bulbs: 3 inches (7.5 cm).

It is often found in the wild and has abundant, narrow, bluish green foliage. Species has one flower to a stem. Spectacular flowering, very suitable for beautiful groups under trees and shrubs and as cut flowers.

Principal variety

ACTAEA: pure white perianth, gold-yellow cup with bright red edge (see photograph on page 93).

Other Species

In this division, species of different types often called "Wild Narcissus" are combined. Among them are many very unusual and not frequently cultivated flowers that are interesting for the amateur gardener. Only few "wild" species are mentioned and it is not always easy to buy the bulbs.

NARCISSUS ASTURIENSIS or MINIMUM

The small NARCISSUS; native of Spain.
Flower color and flowering period: yellow; February-March.
Average plant height: 4 inches (10 cm).
Spacing between bulbs: 2 inches (5 cm).
It is very suitable for rock gardens (see photograph on page 93).

NARCISSUS BULBOCODIUM (Yellow Hoop Petticoat)

Flower color and flowering period: yellow; February-March.
Average plant height: 6 inches (15 cm).
Spacing between bulbs: 2 inches (5 cm).
It is unusual yellow flowers and is very useful for rock gardens. In contrast to other species, the perianth is almost absent and is composed of six greenish yellow, narrow and pointed segments. The yellow flowers are funnel-shaped. The stamens are bent and as long as the crown. It has thin green leaves. This NARCISSUS multiplies by bulblets and seed. There are different types of this NARCISSUS, but the best-known is BULBOCODIUM CONSPICUUS.

NARCISSUS POETICUS "ACTAEA"

NARCISSUS BULBOCODIUM

93

NARCISSUS CAMPERNELLI

synonym: ODORUS

It is very close to NARCISSUS JONQUILLA and has very odiferous flowers, often 2-3 flowers to a stem. The cultivar, 'Flore-Pleno', with double flowers is best-known (see photograph on left). The foliage tends to be broad.

Flower color and flowering period: yellow; March-April.

Average plant height: 6 inches (15 cm).

Spacing between bulbs: 2 inches (5 cm).

Excellent for rock gardens and under trees and shrubs. It does not do well in areas with very dry summers.

NARCISSUS CANALICULATUS

Flower color and flowering period: white perianth with yellow cup; March-April.

Average plant height: 6 inches (15 cm).

Spacing between bulbs: 2 inches (5 cm).

It has very odiferous flowers, usually 5-7 to a stem (see photograph below). The green leaves are rather broad and longer than the stems.

NARCISSUS LOBULARIS
or LOBULARIA

Flower color and flowering period: yellow; March-April.

Average plant height: 8 inches (20 cm).

Spacing between bulbs: 3 inches (7.5 cm).

It has one bright yellow flower with a slightly deeper yellow trumpet per stem.

NARCISSUS CANALICULATUS

NARCISSUS LOBULARIS

NARCISSUS NANUS

Flower color and flowering period: yellow; March.
Average plant height: 6 inches (15 cm).
Spacing between bulbs: 2 inches (5 cm).
It has a bright yellow perianth with a deeper yellow trumpet that is longer than the petals of the perianth (see photograph on right).

NARCISSUS PUMILUS

Flower color and flowering period: yellow; April.
Average plant height: 6 inches (15 cm).
Spacing between bulbs: 3 inches (7.5 cm).
It has large sulphur-yellow flowers with a deeper yellow trumpet. The leaves are small. The cultivar, 'Rip Van Winkle', has double, bright-yellow flowers.

JONQUIL
Narcissus Pseudo-Narcissus

Native to Central and Southern Europe, this real Jonquil is often confused with NARCISSUS JONQUILLA (small Jonquil).
This species is very difficult to find. Growers prefer to raise the horticultural, and more spectacular, cultivars that are easier to grow. The species consists of several varieties of which the best-known are: NARCISSUS PSEUDO-NARCISSUS "MOSCHATUS". It has creamy yellow flowers and is about 8 inches (20 cm) tall.

NARCISSUS PUMILUS

NARCISSUS PSEUDO-NARCISSUS or real jonquil

ORNITHOGALUM NUTANS   ORNITHOGALUM UMBELLATUM

Ornithogalum

Family: Liliaceae

The name is derived from Greek words, Ornis meaning bird and Gala meaning milk. This name probably is related to the white color and elegance of the flowers. The genus consists of about 150 species that are very difficult to classify. Four species are cultivated, two of them summer-flowering and they will be described in another book. ORNITHOGALUM grow well in any well-drained soil. The bulbs prefer to be left in the soil to multiply.

Principal species

ORNITHOGALUM NUTANS

Flower color and flowering period: white inside and greenish outside; April-May.
Average plant height: 12-18 inches (30-45 cm).
Planting depth to base of bulb: 5 inches (12.5 cm)
Spacing between bulbs: 3 inches (7.5 cm).
Light requirements: Full sun to partial shade.
Landscape uses: borders, beds with other bulbous or perennial plants, and rock gardens.
The flowers are star-shaped and nodding on long, strong stems (see photograph above). The leaves are long, narrow (ribbon like) and green-grey silvery in color.

ORNITHOGALUM UMBELLATUM

Star of Bethlehem.
The flowers only open when the sun shines and close when there is no sunlight.
UMBELLATUM originate in Europe, Asia Minor and North Africa.
Flower color and flowering period: white; April-May.
Average plant height: 6 inches (15 cm).
Planting depth to base of bulb: 5 inches (12.5 cm).
Spacing between bulbs: 2 inches (5 cm).
Light requirements: Full sun to partial shade.
Landscape uses: borders and rock gardens.
The white and outside green-striped flowers are united in umbels on strong stems (see photograph above). This species perennializes readily in climatic zones 4-9.

Oxalis adenophylla

Family: Oxalidaceae

The word OXALIS is derived from Greek word, OXIS, meaning acid.
The genus OXALIS consists of hundred of species. Some of them are shrubs, perennials, annuals and some bulbous plants. The leaves have an acid taste. Two of the most widely cultivated species are: OXALIS ADENOPHYLLA and OXALIS DEPPEI. The latter must be planted in spring and flowers in summer and will be described in another book.

Planting and cultivation

Flower color and flowering period: pink; May-July.
Average plant height: 3 inches (7.5 cm).
Planting depth to base of bulb: 5 inches (12.5 cm)
Spacing between bulbs: 3 inches (7.5 cm).
Light requirements: Full sun to partial shade.
Landscape uses: borders and rock gardens.
Native to Chile and Argentina, this winterhardy species grows well in any well-drained soil. It requires an alkaline soil and prefers to be left in the ground to form a thick carpet. The flowers are bright and deep pink with black hearts (see photograph on right). The foliage is deeply lobed, bluish green and very decorative.

OXALIS
ADENOPHYLLA

Puschkinia libanotica

Family: Liliaceae
Common name: PUSCHKINIA
LIBANOTICA

This genus owes its name to the Russian botanist Puschkin. It is native to Asia and the Middle East. Only one species is known and it is very close to the SCILLA'S.

Planting and cultivation

Flower color and flowering period: bluish-white; March-April.
Average plant height: 4 inches (10 cm).
Planting depth to base of bulb: 5 inches (12.5 cm)
Spacing between bulbs: 2 inches (5 cm).
Light requirements: Full sun to partial shade.
Landscape uses: under shrubs and trees, borders and rock gardens.
The bulbs are hardy and should be left in the ground to perennialize. The plant grows well in any, even moist, soil. The flowers, white and bright blue striped, slightly bend the supple stems (see photograph on right). The leaves are long and narrow. The species is an excellent plant for spring. There is also a variety with completely white flowers, PUSCHKINIA LIBANOTICA "ALBA". It is not extensively cultivated.

PUSCHKINIA LIBANOTICA

RANUNCULUS
peony flowering, mixed

Ranunculus

Family: Ranunculaceae

An important genus mainly consisting of perennial, annual, and aquatic species. There is only one bulbous species, RANUNCULUS ASIATICUS. Several hybrids have been bred and all have big double flowers. The cultivation is quite similar to ANEMONE'S. They make very good cut flowers.

Planting and cultivation

Flower color and flowering period: red, yellow, purple, pink, white; May-June.
Average plant height: 12-16 inches (30-40 cm).
Planting depth to base of bulb: 5 inches (12.5 cm)
Spacing between bulbs: 2 inches (5 cm).
Light requirements: Full sun to partial shade.
Landscape uses: fields, beds, borders, and cut flowers.

The bulbs can be planted in the fall or spring. They are not hardy bulbs. That is why spring planting is recommended for climatic zones 4-8. Before planting, the bulbs should be soaked in luke-warm water for about 3-4 hours. If planted in the fall, use a sheltered place. Protect bulbs with a mulch. In regions with mild winters (Climatic Zones 9-10) planting in the fall is recommended. In very mild areas, the bulbs can be left in the soil the year round.
Otherwise, after flowering and senescence of the foliage, the bulbs should be harvested, dried and stored in a dry room. They should be sheltered from frost during the winter. A dry, preferably sandy soil, is preferred for this plant. Depending on the cultivar, the flowers are 2 inches (5 cm) in diameter and are either double or semi-double. The colors range from pure white to deep red (almost black) with all shades in between, except blue and green (see photograph above). The green foliage is little and deeply divided. Ranunculi are offered for sale in mixed assortments and by separate colors.

Principal species

RANUNCULUS GEANTE D'ANJOU
flowers semi-double

RANUNCULUS WITH PEONY FLOWERS
double flowers.

Some firms have raised and commercialized their own "races"; obtained by hybridization of these two species. The flowers are generally bigger and more homogeneous.

Sauromatum guttatum

synonym: ARUM CORNUTUM
Family: Araceae
Common name: Voo Doo bulb

This genus has six species. S. GUTTATUM is native to the Southern Himalayas. This species is known for its disagreeable smell.

Planting and cultivation

Flowering: March to April, when cultivated outdoors.
Height: flower 12-20 inches (30-50 cm); foliage 20-24 inches (50-60 cm).
Cultivation does not present any problem. The very big bulb, 5-6 inches (12.5-15 cm) in diameter, does not need to be planted or watered. It is sufficient to place it on a piece of furniture or window-sill in a room with a temperature of 65-68 °F (18-20 °C). Late in winter a stem develops from the central bud to a height of 12-20 inches (30-50 cm) (see photograph on right).
Subsequently, the greyish stem opens into a spathe - violet purple, brown and yellow spotted - from which emerges the spadix. After a few hours, the curious form of inflorescence spreads a smell of rotten flesh for 2-3 days till the flower has faded. At this time, the plant must be put in the garden or on a balcony to avoid the disagreeable odor inside the house.
Late in April, the bulb can be planted in the garden or in a pot. Plant it about 2 inches (5 cm) deep. Afterwards, a 20-24 inches (50-60 cm) high stem grows an elegant divided foliage develops, giving the plant the aspect of a dwarf palm-tree.. Before the first frost, the bulbs must be kept again inside to start a new vegetative cycle.

SAUROMATUM GUTTATUM bulb and blooming plant

SELAGINELLA completely grown, and as a dry ball

Selaginella

Family: Selaginellaceae
Formerly: Lycopodiaceae
Genus: English moss

Although this is not a bulbous plant, it is included in this book because it is frequently offered for sale as a bulb.
The genus consists of more than 300, herbaceous and always green species similar to moss. SELAGINELLA LEPIDOPHYLLA, the species covered in the book, is native to Peru and Texas.

Planting and cultivation

It is used exclusively as an indoor-plant. It looks like a globulal dry bunch with thin and short roots. It is rather similar to twigs of THUJA.
For regrowth, it is adequate to put the plant with its base on water in a cup or deep plate. Fully grown SELAGINELLA looks like a dwarf conifer with a diameter of about 8-10 inches (20-25 cm). Although it is not very decorative, this curious plant is an excellent introduction for children into the world of plants.

Scilla

Family: Liliaceae

This genus consists of about 100 species. Some of them often classified in different genera, e.g. ENDYMION, but in this book all of them are grouped under SCILLA.

Principal species

SCILLA CAMPANULATA

synonym: SCILLA HISPANICA, HYACIN-THOIDUS HISPANICA, ENDYMION HIS-PANICUS.
Common name: wood hyacinths
Native to Spain and Portugal.
Flower color and flowering period: white, pink, or blue; April-June.
Average plant height: 8-10 inches (20-25 cm).
Planting depth to base of bulb: 5 inches (12.5 cm)
Spacing between bulbs: 3 inches (7.5 cm).
Light requirements: Full sun to partial shade.
Landscape uses: borders, rock gardens and perennial beds.
These Scilla's require a fertile and well-drained soil. They prefer to be left in the ground, in sheltered position, and will flower for many years. The stems are slightly and gracefully bent by the numerous bell-shaped flowers.
The foliage is green and broad.
This species is mostly cultivated and offered for sale in assortments of color (see photograph on page 101). However, some remarkable varieties with bigger flowers are mentioned below.
BLUE GIANT: deep blue
BLUE QUEEN: bright blue
ROSE QUEEN: bright pink
SKY BLUE: bright blue

SCILLA NUTANS

synonym: ENDYMION NON-SCRIPTUS, HYACINTHOIDUS NON-SCRIPTA, 'Bluebell' Native to Spain and Portugal it is not extensively cultivated. It is rather close to the preceding species in shape, color of the flowers and cultivation. It does best, however, under cool shady conditions e.g. in leafy soil under trees and shrubs (see photograph on page 101).

SCILLA SIBERICA

A well known species. It is close to CHIONO-DOXA LUCILAE (Glory of the Snow) and often confused with it. S. SIBERICA is native to Siberia and Caucasus and is very hardy.
Flower color and flowering period: blue; March-April.
Average plant height: 5 inches (12.5 cm).
Planting depth to base of bulb: 5 inches (12.5 cm)
Spacing between bulbs: 1 inch (2.5 cm).
Light requirements: Full sun to partial shade.
Landscape uses: borders, rock gardens and under trees and shrubs.

SCILLA SIBERICA

Species is easy to cultivate. Bulbs can be kept in the ground for many years and naturalize easy. Each bulb produces 3-4 stems with 3-5 bell-shaped flowers (see photograph above). Abundant green foliage appears well before flowering. The main cultivar is violet-blue, but there are some outstanding cultivars:
ALBA: pure white
ATROCAERULEA: deep blue, big flowers
SPRING BEAUTY: vigorous plant with bright blue flowers (see photograph above).

SCILLA TUBERGENIANA

synonym: SCILLA MICZENKOANA
This species is native to Iran. It has been cultivated and commercialized by the firm Van Tubergen of Haarlem, The Netherlands. It is very close to SCILLA SIBERICA, and has very pale blue flowers. Flowers earlier than S. SIBERICA. Very suitable for combinations with ERANTHIS (Winter Aconite) and GALANTHUS (Snowdrops) (see photograph on right).

SCILLA TUBERGENIANA

SCILLA CAMPANULATA

SPARAXIS TRICOLOR

Sparaxis tricolor

Family: Iridaceae

SCILLA NUTANS

This genus, a native of South Africa, has few species and SPARAXIS TRICOLOR is the only one that is cultivated. Like Freesias and Ixias, this plant is not cold hardy. The bulbs offered for sale are mainly hybrids.

Planting and cultivation

Flower color and flowering period: white, orange, red, purple; April-May.
Average plant height: 8-10 inches (20-25 cm).
Planting depth to base of bulb: 5 inches (12.5 cm)
Spacing between bulbs: 2 inches (5 cm).
Light requirements: Full sun.

Landscape uses: fields, beds, borders, rock garden and as cut flowers.
SPARAXIS should be planted in spring in northern climates.
In regions with very mild winters the bulbs can be left in the ground throughout the year.
SPARAXIS requires a sandy, fertile and well-drained soil.
The flowers vary in color from white to purple (almost black) and are mostly spotted (see photograph above). They are borne on spikes on strong stems. They make excellent cut flowers. The foliage is deep green and narrow. SPARAXIS TRICOLOR is almost always offered for sale as mixed colors.

Tecophilaea cyanocrocus

Family: Tecophilaeaceae
Common name: CHILEAN CROCUS

It is native to the dry regions of Chile. This plant has luminous deep blue flowers, but is not extensively cultivated. Thus, the bulbs are rare and expensive.

Planting and cultivation

Flower color and flowering period: blue; March-April.
Average plant height: 5 inches (12.5 cm).
Planting depth to base of bulb: 5 inches (12.5 cm).
Spacing between bulbs: 2 inches (5 cm).
Light requirements: Full sun.
Landscape uses: rock gardens.

It is a very delicate plant. In regions with winters that have freezing temperatures, the bulbs must be planted in pots and kept in a well lighted non-heated room. If plants are in the open, in very mild areas, the bulbs must be well protected, e.g. by plastic, if the weather becomes cold. A well-drained soil is necessary and it needs frequent waterings during the periods of growth and flowering.
Bulbs will slowly multiply when left in the ground. Their life-span is 3-4 years maximum. The little, green, narrow foliage is quite similar to CROCUS. The blue flowers are funnel-shaped. The type with magnificent, blue flowers and a small white heart is easiest to obtain (see photograph above). The varieties "Leichtlinii" with big white centre and blue-edged petals and "Violacea" with deep violet with small white heart are very rare.

Tulipa

Tulipa

Common name: TULIP
Family: Liliaceae

This genus is undoubtedly the most important one covered in this book. This is due to the fact that tulips are cultivated on a very large scale. There are numerous species and cultivars, and they are immensely popular amongst gardeners the world over. The Netherlands ranks first and foremost in the production of tulips. Billions of bulbs and cut flowers are exported annually to a great many countries. Thousands of people comprise the various segments of the tulip "industry". For some information on its introduction to Europe and its very interesting history we refer the reader to the first pages of this book.

Many of the present day cultivars have been developed from TULIPA GESNERIANA by successful cross-breedings not only with various botanical or wild species but also between the new cultivars. More than 3000 cultivars are listed and each year new cultivars are bred and named (see Chapter on Propagation).

Classification

In 1981, the Royal Bulb Growers Association of The Netherlands adopted the following classification of the different species and cultivars of tulips.

The last class consists of all other species and their cultivars and hybrids. They are often cultivated in small quantities. They deserve, however, special attention because of their unique characteristics.

A beautiful combination: FLAMING PARROT lily flowering tulip WEST POINT, and cottage tulip RENOWN

Planting and cultivation

Tulips are hardy bulbs and when properly planted will survive even the severest winters. They grow best in a well-drained soil. Poor drainage can cause poor rooting of the bulbs and it also contributes to the development of diseases. Tulips do well in full sun to partial shade. A well-sheltered position is recommended for the tall varieties to give them protection from strong winds. The planting-period extends from late september till the end of November. The exact time depends on the Climatic Zone. In zones 4-6, they should be planted early and in Zones 7-9 later.

Colors and Flowering period:
Red, Yellow, Pink, Lavender, White, Bicolors; March-May, depending on the cultivar and climatic zone, and they are referred to either as early, medium, or late within the tulip flowering season.

Average plant height: 5-24 inches (12.5-60 cm), depending on the cultivar and climatic zone.

Planting depth to base of bulb: 8 inches (20 cm) for large bulbs; 5 inches (12.5 cm) for small bulbs.

Spacing between bulbs: 2-4 inches (5-10 cm).

Light requirements: Full sun to partial shade.

Landscape uses: Beds, borders, rock gardens and cut flowers.

The principal classes are described and illustrated and only the readily cultivars are mentioned. In addition, examples of most of the types, shapes or colors are illustrated.

Principal classes of Tulips

SINGLE EARLY TULIPS

Flowering period: Early.

Average plant height: 8-12 inches (20-30 cm).

Spacing between bulbs: 2 to 4 inches (5 to 10 cm).

Landscape uses: beds, borders, rock gardens and forcing.

The word single implies that cultivars have only one flower with six petals. They are distinguished from the Double Early Tulips that have well excess of 6 petals and look like peonies. Some of the Single Early Tulips can be used for inside forcing and the cultivars that are particularly suitable are indicated by an asterisk.

Principal varieties

APRICOT BEAUTY*: salmon pink

ARMA: red, fringed petals

BELLONA*: bright yellow

BESTSELLER: bright orange

BRILLIANT STAR MAXIMA*: scarlet

CHARLES*: blood red

CHRISTMAS MARVEL*: deep pink

COULEUR CARDINAL: violet-red

DIANA: white

EARLY LIGHT: bright red

GENERAL DE WET*: orange (sweet-smelling)

GRAND DUC (Keizerskroon)*: red and yellow

IBIS: bright pink and red

JOFFRE*: deep yellow

LUCIDA*: red, yellow edged

MERRY CHRISTMAS*: carmine red, white base

PRINS CARNAVAL: yellow with red flame

PRINCESS IRENE: orange and red

STRIPED BELLONA: yellow and orange

VAN DER NEER: lavender

YOKOHAMA: lemon yellow

* Cultivars that are recommended for forcing.

As with most classes of tulips, mixed colors are available.

YOKOHAMA, one of the most exquisite yellow varieties

VAN DER NEER beautiful violet

PRINS
CARNAVAL

CHARLES

DIANA

PRINCESSE IRENE

CHRISTMAS MARVEL,
excellent for indoor forcing

APRICOT BEAUTY

BELLONA, heavenly scented

COULEUR CARDINAL

CARLTON

DOUBLE EARLY
TULIPS MIXED

DOUBLE EARLY TULIPS

These should not be confused with the Double Late Tulips.

Flowering period: Early.

Average plant height: 8-12 inches (20-30 cm).

Spacing between bulbs: 2 inches (5 cm).

Landscape uses: beds, borders and rock gardens.

A very interesting class. They flower early, have long lasting flowers, strong stems and are short. An excellent class for the garden and the double flowers open flat 3-4 inches (7.5-10 cm) in the full sun. When planted in a compact group, the tulips develop into a magnificent carpet of color.

The color range for double early tulips is a little less than for other classes. For mixed plantings, the 'Murillo' sports* are recommended. They ensure a homogeneity in sizes and shapes of the flowers and period of flowering.

Principal cultivars:

BABY DOLL**: yellow
BRAVISSIMO: red with brown edges
CARLTON: blood red
ELECTRA*: magenta red
ETNA: ruby red, yellow base
HOANGHO: gold yellow
HYTUNA: gold yellow
KAREOL**: deep gold yellow
MONTE CARLO**: sulphur yellow
Mr. VAN DER HOEF*: lemon yellow
ORANGE NASSAU*: deep orange
PEACH BLOSSOM*: tender pink
SCHOONOORD*: pure white
STOCKHOLM* **: bright red
TRIUMPHATOR: bright pink
WILLEM OF ORANGE: orange, flushed copper red
WILLEMSOORD*: red, white edged

* = Murillo sports.
** = Excellent for forcing.

As with most classes of tulips, mixed colors are available.

WILLEMSOORD

ELECTRA

ORANGE NASSAU

DOUBLE EARLY TULIPS MIXED

Mr VAN DER HOEFF

STOCKHOLM

WILLEM OF ORANGE

PEACH BLOSSOM

JIMMY

ALBURY

TRIUMPH TULIPS

Triumph tulips are a very important class. There is a large number of cultivars and, thus, a wide array of colors available. Most of the Triumph Tulips have been obtained by cross-breeding Single Early Tulips with Single Late Tulips.

Flowering period: Medium.
Average plant height: 10-16 inches (25-40 cm).
Spacing between bulbs: 2 to 4 inches (5 to 10 cm).
Landscape uses: beds, borders, cut flowers, and forcing.

The cup-shaped flowers are borne on strong stems and they stand up well under poor weather conditions. Many cultivars are produced not only for the garden but also for forcing. They make excellent cut flowers.

Principal varieties
ABRA*: mahogany red, yellow edge
ABU HASSAN: purple brown, yellow-edged
ADORNO: luminous deep orange
ALBURY: currant-red, blueish green base
ANTWERP: carmine red, yellow base
ARABIAN MISTERY: violet, white edged
ATTILA: purple violet
BELCANTO: cardinal red, small yellow edge
BING CROSBY*: brilliant scarlet
BLENDA*: carmine red, white base
BLUE BELL: purple, violet, white base
CASSINI*: blood red
CORIOLAN: deep red, yellow edged
DON QUICHOTTE: deep pink
DREAMING MAID: violet, white edged
DUTCH PRINCESS: yellow edged orange
FIDELIO*: orange yellow and red
FRANKFURT: cardinal red, yellow base
GARDEN PARTY: white and carmine red
GOLDEN MELODY*: bright yellow
GOLDEN MIRJORAN*: carmine pink, yellow edged

HIBERNIA*: pure white
HIGH SOCIETY: orange-red, orange-edged
HUGO SCHLOSSER: scarlet red
INVASION: deep red, creamy-edged
INZELL*: ivory white
JIMMY: luminous orange
KANSAS: pure white
KEES NELIS*: bright red, broad yellow edge
LUCKY STRIKE: bright red, white edged
MAKASSAR: deep yellow
MEISSNER PORZELLAN: pink and white
MERRY WIDOW*: red, white edged
MIRJORAN*: bordeaux red and creamy yellow
MISS HOLLAND: blood red, yellow base
MUSICAL: cardinal red, black base
NEGRITA: deep blue-violet
ORANGE MONARCH*: orange and red
ORANGE WONDER: orange
ORNAMENT: yellow
PARIS: red, yellow edge
PAUL RICHTER*: bright red
PAX*: pure white
PEERLESS PINK: tender pink
PRELUDIUM*: carmine pink, white base
PRINCE CHARLES*: purple-violet
PRINCESS BEATRIX: red and orange, gold-yellow edged
PROMINENCE*: deep red
PURPLE STAR: violet purple
REFORMA: bright yellow
ROSARIO: magenta pink, white base
SNOWFLAKE: creamy and greyish white
SNOWSTAR*: pure white
TAMBOUR MAITRE: deep red
THULE*: yellow and red
TOLEDO: currant red, yellow edged
VALENTINE: purple pink, whitish edge
WHITE DREAM: ivory white
WONDERLAND: yellow, flamed red

* Cultivars that are recommended for forcing.

As with most class of tulips, mixed colors are available.

PRELUDIUM

FIDELIO, lovely color, unusual form

PURPLE STAR

WONDERLAND

LUCKY STRIKE

THULE

TAMBOUR MAÎTRE, wonderful garden variety

112

ATTILA the best of the violet colors

PARIS

DON QUICHOTTE

ORANGE WONDER

REFORMA

ARABIAN MYSTERY

KANSAS

GARDEN PARTY

ABU HASSAN

ANTWERP

DUTCH PRINCESS

PEERLESS PINK

PRINCE CHARLES

BING CROSBY

MEISSNER PORZELLAN

KEES NELIS

SINGLE LATE TULIPS

This class now consists of the Breeder, Darwin and Cottage Tulips that were combined. All cultivars flower late in the tulip season and have long and strong stems. Along with the Darwin Hybrids, they are amongst the tallest Tulips for the garden. The colors range from red, yellow, orange, pink, white to unusual bicolored cultivars. The "Viridiflora" and "Fringed" (Crispa) were previously considered as 'single late Tulips', but they are now separate classes. They will be described on separate pages.

Flowering period: Late
Average plant height: 14-30 inches (35-75 cm).
Spacing between bulbs: 3 inches (7.5 cm).
Landscape uses: parks, beds, perennial beds and cut-flowers.

Principal varieties:
ADVANCE: light scarlet
ALABASTER: pure white
ARISTOCRAT: bright pink and red
ASTA NIELSEN: sulphur yellow
AVIGNON: bright red
BALALAIKA: blood red
BLEU AIMABLE: deep violet blue
CANTOR: coral pink
CASHMIR: bright red
CORDELL HULL: red and white
DEMETER: purple violet
DILLENBURG: orange, flamed yellow
DUKE OF WELLINGTON: pure white
ESTHER: light magenta
GANDER: magenta red
GANDER'S RHAPSODY: red and white
GOLDEN HARVEST: gold yellow
GRAND STYLE: deep red
GREUZE: deep lavender
HALCRO: bright red
ILE DE FRANCE: cardinal red
KING'S BLOOD: carmine and vermillion red
LANDSEADEL'S SUPREME: deep red
MAGIER: white, violet-blue veined
MAMASSA: bright yellow

QUEEN OF NIGHT

MAMASSA

ARISTOCRAT, a well-chosen name

SWEET HARMONY, 'butter and cream' tulip

CUM LAUDE

CORDELL HULL

ADVANCE

PICTURE, very unusual form

SINGLE LATE TULIPS

MAUREEN: ivory-white
MONTGOMERY: white with red spots
MOST MILES: bright red
Mrs. JOHN T. SCHEEPERS: bright yellow
PANDION: violet-blue, white edged
PICTURE: rose
PINK DIAMOND: tender pink
PINK SUPREME: luminous deep pink
PRINCESS MARGARET ROSE: yellow and red
RENOWN: bright pink
QUEEN OF BARTIGONS: salmon-pink
QUEEN OF NIGHT: purple-black
SHIRLEY: ivory-white, purple edge
SMILING QUEEN: tender pink
SORBET: white and magenta pink flamed
SUNKIST: gold-yellow
SWEET HARMONY: lemon-yellow, white edge
TEMPLE OF BEAUTY: salmon orange
TWINKLE: white, flamed red
UNION JACK: creamy white and red
VLAMMENSPEL: yellow, flamed red

As with most classes of tulips, mixed colors are available.

GOLDEN HARVEST

BALALAÏKA

PRINCESS MARGARET ROSE   HALCRO

TEMPLE OF BEAUTY®

GRAND STYLE
120   GREENLAND, a viridiflora tulip

RENOWN

VLAMMENSPEL

SORBET, a melting color

MAUREEN

DILLENBURG

TWINKLE

121

DARWIN HYBRID TULIPS

This is a rather recent tulip class developed by the Dutch tulip breeders. Mr. D. W. Lefeber of Lisse, The Netherlands was one of the prominent breeders of this class. These Tulips have been obtained by cross-breeding the famous TULIPA FOSTERIANA Madame Lefeber (Red Emperor) and cultivars of Darwin Tulips. Their cultivation is very easy and gardeners will derive a lot of enjoyment from this class of tulips. They have perfectly shaped flowers and are amongst the biggest of all Tulips. Also, they have strong stems. Because of these characteristics, these Tulips are widely used as cut-flowers and are forced in enormous quantities. Due to the abundant, vigorous, glaucous-green foliage, it is an excellent class for large plants in fields, parks, and flower-beds. The very luminous and brilliant colors are limited to shades of red, orange, pink and yellow, but they often have spots or stripes.

Flowering period: Medium
Average plant height: 12-20 inches (30-50 cm).
Spacing between bulbs: 3 inches (7.5 cm).
Landscape uses: park beds, perennial beds, borders and cut-flowers.

Principal varieties
AD REM: deep orange
APELDOORN: brilliant vermillion red
APELDOORN'S ELITE: red and orange-yellow
BEAUTY OF APELDOORN: orange-yellow, red striped
BIG CHIEF: bright pink with silver-white striped
DIPLOMAT: vermillion red
DOVER: carmine and vermillion red
ELIZABETH ARDEN: salmon pink (low variety, 25 cm)
FRINGED APELDOORN: bright red, fringed petals
GENERAL EISENHOWER: vermillion
GOLDEN APELDOORN: lemon-yellow
GOLDEN OXFORD: bright yellow
GOLDEN PARADE: bright yellow, red lined edges
GOLDEN DEUTSCHLAND: gold-yellow
GORDON COOPER: bright magenta red
GUDOŞHNIK: bright yellow, red striped
HANS MAYER: gold-yellow, red flamed

HOLLAND'S GLORY: luminous bright orange
JEWEL OF SPRING: lemon yellow
LEFEBER'S FAVOURITE: brilliant carmine red
LONDON: blood red, scarlet hued
OLYMPIC FLAME: yellow, red flamed
ORANGE SUN: deep orange
OXFORD: vermillion red
OXFORD ELITE: red and orange yellow
PARADE: bright red
PRESIDENT KENNEDY: gold-yellow, red lined edges
RED MATADOR: blood red
SPRING SONG: bright red
STRIPED APELDOORN: gold yellow, red striped
VIVEX: bright orange
YELLOW DOVER: buttercup yellow

As with most classes of tulips, mixed colors are available.

BEAUTY OF APELDOORN

GOLDEN APELDOORN

APELDOORN'S ELITE

GUDOSHNIK

ELIZABETH ARDEN

AD REM

BIG CHIEF, an elegant tulip with a bright rose color

OLYMPIC FLAME

OXFORD

JEWEL OF SPRING

STRIPPED APELDOORN

ORANGE SUN

GORDON COOPER

VIVEX

Large flowers, strong stems make the Darwin Hybrid an ideal cut flower.

SPRING SONG

LILY-FLOWERING TULIPS

These Tulips with long reflexed petals are borne on strong stems. They are highly suited for cut flower usage. The leaves are narrower than those of the other Tulips. Compared with other classes, there are relatively few varieties.

Flowering period: Late.
Average plant height: 14-30 inches (35-75 cm).
Spacing between bulbs: 2 inches (5 cm).
Landscape uses: park beds, borders, perennial beds and cut-flowers.

Principal varieties:
ALADDIN: deep red, yellow edged
BALLADE: bright violet, white edged
BURGUNDY: deep purple-violet
CHINA PINK: luminous carmine pink
ELEGANT LADY: creamy-yellow, edged violet-red
JACQUELINE: tender pink
MARIETTE: pure pink
MAYTIME: bright violet, white edged
QUEEN OF SHEBA: red, yellow edged
RED SHINE: bright red
WEST POINT: bright yellow
WHITE TRIUMPHATOR: pure white

As with most classes of tulips mixed colors are available.

BALLADE

WHITE TRIUMPHATOR

CHINA PINK

RED SHINE

JACQUELINE   QUEEN OF SHEBA   MAYTIME

ELEGANT LADY

BURGUNDY   WEST POINT   MARIETTE

FLAMING PARROT, just like a brightly colored parrot

RED PARROT

ESTELLA RIJNVELD

PARROT TULIPS

This class of Tulips is well-known for its unusual feather-like flowers, with spots and chiselled petals. The majority of the cultivars originate as mutations from Single Late and Triumph Tulips. Depending on the cultivars, the petals are more or less incised. Whatever the colors may be (single or multicolored), most flowers have a green spot in the middle base of the petals. Until the flowers begin coloring, they are almost completely bright green and this may be deceptive for those who grow these Tulips for the first time. Parrot Tulips have very big flowers on supple stems. They are particularly sensitive to poor weather-conditions. Therefore, they should be planted in protected areas. In the sun, the flowers open almost horizontally and a star-shaped black heart appears from which emerges the bright yellow pistil. The foliage is rich, vigorous, and blueish green.

Flowering period: Medium to Late.
Average plant height: 14-20 inches (35-50 cm).
Spacing between bulbs: 3 inches (7.5 cm).
Landscape uses: beds, borders and cut-flowers.

Principal varieties
APRICOT PARROT: bright apricot-colored, pink striped
BIRD OF PARADISE: brown red, orange edged
BLACK PARROT: violet black
BLUE PARROT: mauve blue
ERNA LINDGREEN: brilliant red
ESTELLA RIJNVELD: red and cream-white
FANTASY: bright pink
FLAMING PARROT: yellow and red
KAREL DOORMAN: red, small yellow edge
ORANGE FAVOURITE: bright orange
RED CHAMPION: blood red
RED PARROT: brilliant blood red
SALMON PARROT: salmon, yellow striped
TEXAS FLAME: yellow and red
TEXAS GOLD: bright yellow
WHITE PARROT: pure white

As with most classes of tulips, mixed colors are available.

KAREL DOORMAN   WHITE PARROT   BIRD OF PARADISE

TEXAS GOLD

BLACK PARROT   FANTASY   ORANGE FAVOURITE

129

DOUBLE LATE (PEONY) TULIPS

This class of Tulips has relatively few cultivars. They are, however, especially interesting because of their double flowers that are quite similar to Peonies. The big flowers are particularly sensitive to severe rain and wind weather-conditions. Therefore, they should be planted in a protected area. They make excellent cut flowers just as they begin to open.

Flowering period: Late
Average plant height: 12-16 inches (30-40 cm).
Spacing between bulbs: 3 inches (7.5 cm).
Landscape uses: beds, borders, and cut flowers.

Principal varieties
ALLEGRETTO: red, yellow edged
ANGELIQUE*: pink, white-pink edged
BONANZA: deep red, yellow edged
GERBRAND KIEFT: red, white edged
KASTRUP: blood and carmine red
MAY WONDER: bright pink
MOUNT TACOMA: cream white
NIZZA: yellow and red
UNCLE TOM: blackish maroon
WIROSA*: bordeaux red, cream edged

* Excellent cultivars for forcing.

As with most classes of tulips, mixed colors are available.

Attractive mixture of double late flowering tulips

NIZZA

GERBRAND KIEFT

130

BONANZA

Garden group of double flowering late tulips

REMBRANDT TULIPS

The antique Rembrandt tulips were very popular. Their origin was the Darwin tulips, the colors of which were modified by several kinds of viruses.

Fantastic prices were paid for these tulips in the 17th. and 18th. Century. People then did not know that the Color variations were caused by virus affections.

At the present time the original Rembrandt tulips are not cultivated anymore.

The antique Rembrandt tulip, just as they used to be produced

GEORGETTE

ORANGE BOUQUET

TULIPS - MULTIFLOWERED

This is not an official class of Tulips. It is a collection of cultivars that have as their principal flowering characteristic, a multiflowering habit. That is, the main stem branches into secondary stems each having one flower. Based on the cultivar and the size of the bulb, a plant may produce 3-7 flowers.

Multiflowered tulips vary greatly in plant height and the size of the flowers.

1. Cultivars belonging to the Single Late Tulips Class

The flower on the main stem is about as large as that of the Single Late Tulips, while those of the secondary stems are slightly smaller. They are useful as cut flowers and very suitable in combination with shorter plants.

Flowering period: Late.

Average plant height: 14-30 inches (35-75 cm).

Spacing between bulbs: 3 inches (7.5 cm).

Landscape uses: parks, beds, borders, and cutflowers.

Principal varieties

GEORGETTE: yellow, red spotted

KEUKENHOF: scarlet red

ORANGE BOUQUET: luminous orange

RED BOUQUET: bright red

TORONTO, perfect for flower beds and border groups

KEUKENHOF

2. *Cultivars belonging to the Botanic Tulip Classes*
GREIGII TULIPS
These plants have the same characteristics as the single flowered GREIGII tulips.

Principal varieties
CAPTEIN'S FAVOURITE: vermillion red, foliage spotted
COMPOSTELLA: vermillion red and gold yellow
GEORGE EASTMAN: vermillion red with gold edges, foliage spotted
TORONTO: bright salmon pink, foliage spotted.

PRAESTANS TULIPS
These are very popular Tulips. They have small flowers, abundant foliage, and are especially beautiful in large groups. The bulbs can be kept in the ground for several years, where they perennialize to form magnificent carpets of flowers.

Flowering period: Early.
Average plant height: 8-10 inches (20-25 cm).
Spacing between bulbs: 3 inches (7-5 cm).
Landscape uses: parks, beds, and perennial beds.

Principal varieties
PRAESTANS FUSILIER: luminous vermillion red
PRAESTANS UNICUM: orange-red, green with yellow edged leaves
PRAESTANS VAN TUBERGEN'S VARIETY: luminous vermillion red
PRAESTANS ZWANENBURG VARIETY: luminous bright red.

The two first varieties are improvements of the Praestans VAN TUBERGEN'S variety with more and bigger flowers and greater plant vigor. The Dutch firms Van Tubergen and Konijenburg and Mark are specialists in the production of multiflowered Tulips. Others exist, but they are more difficult to obtain.

PRAESTANS UNICUM,
with extremely decorative leaves

133

Fringed or CRISPA TULIPS in an attractive mixture

FRINGED TULIPS

This is a special class of Tulips and all the culti-vars have slightly incised (fringed) petals. This relatively new type of flower is becoming very popular. This is due to their elegance and long flower-life. Many of them are mutants of the Single Late Tulips.

Flowering period: Late.
Average plant height: 8-30 inches (20-75 cm).
Spacing between bulbs: 2 inches (5 cm).
Landscape uses: parks, beds, and cut-flowers.

Principal cultivars
1./ Mutants from Single Late Tulips
BELL FLOWER: mauve pink
BLUE HERON: purple violet
BURGUNDY LACE: deep carmine red
MAJA: gold yellow

As with most class of tulips, mixed colors are available.

2./ Mutants from Darwin Hybrid Tulips
FRINGED APELDOORN: vermillion red
FRINGED OXFORD: vermillion red
FRINGED ELEGANCE: bright yellow

3./ Mutants from Single Early Tulips
ARMA: cardinal red.

4./ Mutants from Double Early Tulips
FRINGED BEAUTY: red with golden-yellow margin

ARMA

FRINGED BEAUTY

VIRIDIFLORA TULIPS

The class is not extensively cultivated. Most of them are related to Single Late Tulips and appreciated by gardeners because of their unusual flower characteristics. As their name indicates the main color of the flowers is green. This is an attractive and rare characteristic amongst flowers. They are also known for their exceptionally long flowering capability. The other characteristics are similar to the Single Late Tulip, except the shapes of the flower are more similar to the Lily-Flowered Tulips. The green part of the flower mostly shows a more or less broad stripe from the base to the terminating point of the petals. They are very suitable as cut flowers.

Flowering period: Late.
Average plant height: 16-24 inches (40-60 cm).
Spacing between bulbs: 2 inches (5 cm).
Landscape uses: beds, borders, and cut-flowers

Principal varieties

ARTIST*: deep orange and green
ESPERANTO*: blood red and green, foliage yellow edged
FORMOSA: light yellow and green
GOLDEN ARTIST*: gold yellow and green
GROENLAND: pink and green
HOLLYWOOD*: blood red and green
HUMMING BIRD: yellow and green
RED PIMPERNEL: purple red and green
SHOW BUSINESS: red and green
SPRING-GREEN: ivory white and green

* = shortest cultivars.

The most cultivated of the Viridiflora Tulips is Groenland (Greenland see page 120).

SHOW BUSINESS

ESPERANTO,
new variety with striped leaf

SPRING-GREEN

FRINGED APELDOORN

HUMMING BIRD

ARTIST

KAUFMANNIANA TYPE

Both photos show the opening and closing of the flowers and the natural spread of the botanical tulip.
This is a small group of 'Heart's Delight' flowering in the second year after planting.
The smallest flowers come from the young bulbs grown after the first year of plantation.

KAUFMANNIANA TULIPS
(Botanical Tulips)

The Tulips of this class have been developed from the TULIPA KAUFMANNIANA species, which is native to Turkestan. It was introduced into Europe by the Dutch firm Van Tubergen and the original variety is still being cultivated. As with all cultivars of botanical tulips, the colors are limited to white, yellow, pink, red and intermediary shades. Depending on the cultivar, the foliage is plain blueish green or chocolate brown striped. The stems are very short.

The flowers open in sunlight to form an almost flat hexagonal star. The inside of the flowers, except the plain red varieties, is mostly brighter than the outside which is often white. The open flowers present a beautifully contrasting yellow

or black heart. They are very well-suited for rock gardens and are early flowering. The bulbs can be kept in the ground, where they easily multiply. The comparative photos above illustrate two of the essential qualities of the TULIPA KAUFMANNIANA, in particular, and of the botanical Tulips in general. These photos, taken 4 hours apart, show the flowers closed (upper photo) and then opening in sunlight (lower photo). The natural multiplication of the bulbs is also seen. The smallest flowers are those of small bulbs produced by bulbs planted about 18 months earlier. They had already flowered in the preceding spring.

Flowering period: Early.
Average plant height: 4-8 inches (10-20 cm).
Spacing between bulbs: 3 inches (7.5 cm).
Landscape uses: beds, borders, and rock gardens

THE FIRST

SHOWWINNER

EARLY HARVEST, very early flowering   GOUDSTUK

Principal varieties

KAUFMANNIANA "TYPE": cream white, slightly red striped, green foliage

ALFRED CORTOT: bright red, foliage spotted

ANCILLA: bright and deep pink, green foliage

BERLIOZ: canary yellow, red-veined, foliage spotted

CHOPIN: vermillion red, yellow edged, foliage spotted

CORONA: orange red, foliage spotted

DAYLIGHT: scarlet-red, foliage spotted

EARLY HARVEST: geranium red, yellow edged, foliage spotted (very early)

FAIR LADY: bright red, cream-edged, foliage spotted

FASHION: scarlet red, green foliage

GIUSEPPE VERDI: carmine red, yellow edged, foliage spotted

GLUCK: carmine red, bright yellow edged, foliage spotted

GOUDSTUK (GOLD COIN): carmine red, yellow edged, green foliage

HEART'S DELIGHT: carmine red, pale pink edged, foliage spotted

JEANTINE: vermillion red, apricot edged, foliage spotted

JOHANN STRAUSS: currant red, pale yellow edged, foliage spotted

LOVE SONG*: bright orange, foliage spotted

SCARLET BABY: scarlet red, green foliage

SHAKESPEARE: carmine red, salmon edged, green foliage

SHOWWINNER: cardinal red, foliage spotted

STRESA: curant red and yellow, foliage spotted

THE FIRST: carmine red and ivory-white, green foliage (very early)

As with most classes of tulips, Kaufmanniana's are offered in mixed colors.

SHAKESPEARE

HEART'S DELIGHT

GLUCK

SCARLET BABY

138

ANCILLA, the original waterlily tulip

CONCERTO

CHOPIN

JEANTINE, lovely color

BERLIOZ

FOSTERIANA TULIPS
(Botanical Tulips)

The cultivars of this class are hybrids developed from the tulips native to the mountains of Central Asia. They vary in heights from 10-20 inches (25 to 50 cm). The large foliage is sometimes spotted. All cultivars are vigorous and the bulbs can be left in the ground, where they multiply easily. One of the most famous Tulips (Red Emperor or Madame Lefeber) which has a beautiful, shining fire-red color belongs to this class.

Flowering period: Early.
Average plant height: 10-20 inches (25-50 cm).
Spacing between bulbs: 4 inches (10 cm).
Landscape uses: park beds, borders, and rock gardens.

Principal varieties
CANDELA: lemon yellow
CANTATA*: vermillion red beautiful shining bronze-green foliage
CONCERTO: sulfur-white
EASTER PARADE: bright red and yellow
GALATA: fire red, yellow base
GOLDEN EAGLE: orange, yellow edged
HIT PARADE: mimosa yellow, red flamed
JUAN: luminous deep orange, yellow base, foliage with brown spots
ORANGE EMPEROR: bright orange, yellow base
PINKEEN (Pink Emperor): pink and red, yellow base
PRINCEPS*: bright red, bronze green base
RED EMPEROR (Madame Lefeber): luminous fire-red
REGINALD DIXON: bright red, yellow edged
PURISSIMA (White Emperor): pure white
RONDO: vermillion red, gold yellow edged
SPRING PEARL: bright pink, vermillion luster
TENDER BEAUTY: cream, carmine pink edged
YELLOW EMPEROR: gold-yellow
YELLOW PURISSIMA: gold-yellow
ZOMBIE: carmine red, yellow edged

* = shortest cultivars.

As with many classes of tulips, Fosteriana's are offered in mixed color.

PURISSIMA   PINKEEN

ORANGE EMPEROR

CANDELA, a well chosen name

SPRING PEARL

An attractive bed of PEACOCK TULIPS

MARGARE
HERBST

GREIGII TULIPS
(Botanical Tulips)

TULIPS GREIGII is native to Turkestan. From the native species, numerous hybrids have been obtained. They have bright colors, often spotted; but are always red, yellow, white and the intermediary tints, as is the case for all botanical hybrids. The heights vary from 8-12 inches (20 to 30 cm). The stems are rigid and have medium-sized flowers opening out wide in the sun to reveal a deep colored, often black heart. The leaves are almost always purple-striped or marked. This makes them very attractive in the garden. The bulbs prefer to be left in the ground to multiply naturally and to form compact groups for later flowering. One of the most popular Botanical Tulips 'Red Riding Hood' belongs to this class.

Flowering period: Early.

Average plant height: 8-12 inches (20-30 cm).

Spacing between bulbs: 4 inches (10 cm).

Landscape uses: park beds, borders, and rock gardens.

142

PLAISIR, a much in demand variety

Principal varieties

ALBION STAR: clear yellow shining red
ALI BABA: deep pink, foliage spotted
CAPE COD: apricot, yellow edged, foliage spotted
CORSAGE: salmon pink, yellow edged, foliage spotted
DOCTOR VAN HESTEREN: tangerine red, foliage spotted
DREAM BOAT: luminous salmon, foliage spotted
ENGADIN: bright red, yellow edged, foliage spotted
GOLDEN DAY: golden yellow, red marked foliage spotted
JOLI COEUR: vermillion red and bright pink, white edged, foliage spotted
KING'S ORB: bright red and gold yellow, foliage spotted
LARGE COPPER: vermillion red, violet marked, foliage spotted
MARCH OF TIME: bright red, foliage spotted
MARGARET HERBST*: (Royal Splendour) vermillion red, beautiful, spotted foliage
MARY ANN: magenta red, pale yellow edged, foliage spotted
MELODY D'AMOUR*: yellow and red, foliage spotted
ORANGE ELITE: salmon, orange edged, foliage spotted
ORATORIO: magenta pink, foliage spotted
ORIENTAL BEAUTY: carmine red, foliage spotted
ORIENTAL SPLENDOUR*: carmine red, yellow edged, foliage spotted
PANDOUR: pale yellow, flamed red
PLAISIR: carmine red, white edged, foliage spotted
PRINCESS CHARMANTE*: fire red, enormous, sweet-smelling flowers, shining and spotted foliage. Very remarkable variety
QUEEN INGRID: red, cream yellow edged, foliage spotted
RED REFLECTION: fire red, green foliage
RED RIDING HOOD: shining vermillion red, foliage spotted
RED SURPRISE: scarlet red, foliage spotted
ROCKERY MASTER: bright salmon pink, foliage spotted
SPARKLING FIRE: fire red, foliage spotted
SUN DANCE: vermillion red, yellow edged, foliage spotted
SWEET LADY: salmon pink, foliage spotted
TARAFA: mauve pink, yellow edged, foliage spotted
TREASURE: orange red, carmine tinted, orange-edged, foliage spotted
YELLOW DAWN: old rose, yellow edged, foliage spotted
ZAMPA: pale yellow, red marked, foliage spotted

* = tallest cultivars.

The best-known varieties are often sold in a mixture called 'Peacock'.

DREAM BOAT

CAPE COD,
lovely, two-colored, strong type

PRINCEPS

ALBION STAR

SWEET LADY

ZAMPA

144

ORIENTAL SPLENDOUR

RED RIDING HOOD,
One of the most popular
Greigii Tulips.
Ideal for garden
and windowbox.

ORANGE ELITE, stunning salmon-orange

ENGADIN

145

TREASURE

ORATORIO

PRINCESSE CHARMANTE®,
very lovely variety with large,
heavenly scented flowers.

GOLDEN DAY

TULIPA BAKERI "LILAC WONDER"

TULIPA CLUSIANA 'CYNTHIA' in a flower bed arrangement

TULIPA CHRYSANTHA

TULIPA ACUMINATA

Other Botanical (Species) Tulips

Botanical Tulips, each corresponding to a separate species, are included in this class of Tulips. Only the most spectacular and most readily available species are mentioned. They are rarely ever planted in large quantities. Their main feature is their uniqueness. The bulb enthusiast will always be proud to have them among their collection of bulbs. All are very suitable for rock gardens, borders and small groups. The bulbs prefer to be left in the ground to multiply naturally. Usually, these bulbs are smaller than those of other species. The sizes varying from 6/8 cm to 8/10 cm.

TULIPS ACUMINATA (cornuta)

A very old species with unusual flowers. They are long and narrow and yellow and red marbled (see photograph on left). The petals terminate in fringed points. The foliage is narrow and pale green.
Flowering period: Medium
Average plant height: 16-20 inches (40-50 cm).
Spacing between bulbs: 2 inches (5 cm).

TULIP BAKERI "Lilac Wonder"

A recent variety developed from TULIPA BAKERI. The small lilac-pink flowers open wide out in stars and show a broad orange-yellow heart white edged (see photograph above).
Flowering period: Medium.
Average plant height: 6-8 inches (15-20 cm).
Spacing between bulbs: 3 inches (7.5 cm).

TULIP BATALINII

Native to Turkestan, this species has produced a cultivar "Bronze Charm". It is practically the only one cultivated. The flowers have pointed petals and they are star-shaped when open. The gold yellow color is red-hued (see photograph on page 149). The foliage is narrow and bright green.
Flowering period: Medium.
Average plant height: 6 inches (15 cm).
Spacing between bulbs: 2 inches (5 cm).

TULIP CHRYSANTHA (STELLATA)

This species is native to the mountains of Afghanistan. It can be found there at an altitude of 3000 m. The small flowers are yellow or red. The foliage is blueish-green and very narrow. The variety "Cynthia" has bigger ruby-red and greenish yellow flowers (see photograph above).
Flowering period: Medium.
Average plant height: 6-8 inches (15-20 cm).
Spacing between bulbs: 2 inches (5 cm).

TULIP CLUSIANA (PEPPERMINT STICK)

This is a very old species and is native to Persia and Afghanistan. The supple stems have broad flowers, in red shades of colors, pink-white vertically striped (see photograph on page 149). When the flower is open the pointed petals form an elegant star (see photograph on page 149).
Flowering period: Medium.
Average plant height: 12-14 inches (30-35 cm).
Spacing between bulbs: 3 inches (7.5 cm).

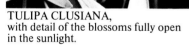
TULIPA CLUSIANA,
with detail of the blossoms fully open
in the sunlight.

TULIP EICHLERI

Native to the mountains of the Caucasus, this
Tulip has big flowers. They are red and yellow
striped and the petals terminate in points (see
photograph on right). The inside shows a black
blotch with yellow crown. It has ample blueish
green foliage. A vigorous plant, it multiplies
rapidly.

Flowering period: Early.
Average plant height: 10-12 inches (25-30 cm).
Spacing between bulbs: 3 inches (7.5 cm).

TULIP KOLPAKOWSKIANA

Species is native to Turkestan. It has small yellow flowers, red flushed (see photograph
above). In full sun it is star-like. The supple
stems sometimes have two flowers.

Flowering period: Medium.
Average plant height: 6-8 inches (15-20 cm).
Spacing between bulbs: 3 inches (7.5 cm).

TULIPA BATALINII

TULIPA EICHLERI

TULIP LINIFOLIA

Native to South Russia, this species has big flowers. They are a brilliant and shining red, almost fluorescent (see photograph above). This is a color not found amongst any other species of tulips. The pointed petals open in the sun, curving back to form an elegant chalice with a brilliant black heart. The narrow, blueish green, linear leaves rosette around the stem.

Flowering period: Late.
Average plant height: 4-6 inches (10-15 cm).
Spacing between bulbs: 3 inches (7.5 cm).

TULIP MARJOLETTI

Species is native to Savoy. The flowers have pointed petals and are yellow and bright red flamed (see photograph on page 151). The foliage is long, narrow and greyish green.

Flowering period: Late.
Average plant height: 20-24 inches.
Spacing between bulbs: 3 inches (7.5 cm).

TULIP PULCHELLA VIOLACEA

synonym: TULIP HUMILIS

Native to Asia Minor, this dwarf species has big globular flowers that open to stars. The color is purple violet with a blue and black base (see photograph on page 151). The narrow foliage is sometimes red edged. Because it is very short, it is an excellent species for rock gardens. It prefers to be planted in a sheltered place.

Flowering period: Early.
Average plant height: 5-6 inches (12.5-15 cm).
Spacing between bulbs: 8-10 cm.

TULIP SAXATILIS

Native to Crete, this species multiplies rapidly and the foliage tends to be rampant. The flowers are mauve pink with a pale yellow base (see photograph below). In the sun, they open wide to form elegant stars on supple stems.

Flowering period: Early.
Average plant height: 12-14 inches (30-40 cm).
Spacing between bulbs: 3 inches (7.5 cm).

TULIPA TARDA (Dasystemon)

Native to Turkestan, it is one of the most interesting species in the group of Botanical Tulips. It multiplies rapidly into compact groups and has abundant, narrow, deep green foliage. Each stem has 5-6 flowers and are star-shaped when open. The petals are gold yellow with a white point (see photograph on page 151). It is a real carpeting plant.

Flowering period: Early.
Average plant height: 4-5 inches (12.5-15 cm).
Spacing between bulbs: 2 inches (5 cm).

TULIP TURKESTANICA

It is native to Turkestan. It is similar to TULIPA TARDA, but the petals are more pointed. The flowers are white and cream when open and have a very decorative black and red heart. Each stems has 7-9 flowers and narrow blueish green leaves. It multiplies rapidly into compact groups.

Flowering period: Early.
Average plant height: 8-10 inches (20-25 cm).
Spacing between bulbs: 2 inches (5 cm).

TULIP URUMIENSIS

It is one of the shortest dwarf Tulips. The bright yellow flowers open in the sun (see photograph on page 151). Unfortunately, this species is not vigorous and it may wear out easily.

Flowering period: Late.
Average plant height: 2-3 inches (5-7.5 cm).
Spacing between bulbs: 2 inches (5 cm).

TULIPA PULCHELLA VIOLACEA

TULIPA URUMIENSIS

TULIPA TARDA, exquisite group, with detail of blossom

TULIPA MARJOLETTI

151

Tulip production field in the region of Hillegom

Propagation of bulbs and development of new cultivars

This chapter is intended to familiarize the gardener's with some of the different stages of development and the handling procedures that bulbs go through before they are sold commercially. The various techniques are described only briefly so that the reader should not expect to get enough information to enable him/her to apply all of them. Propagation of some bulbs, e.g. hyacinths, and especially the breeding of new cultivars is a complicated matter requiring special techniques, years of experience and knowledge.

Nevertheless, the reader may be tempted to try to multiply some rare and expensive species or cultivars. Perhaps, he/she only wishes to get a greater number of bulbs for a more extensive planting or to challenge themselves as a home gardener.

Propagation

There are two main propagation systems; sexual (seeds) and asexual (both natural and artificial). Several techniques of multiplication are used depending on the genera or species.

In principle, all species produce seeds by which bulb increases or new cultivars can be derived. Propagation by seeds, however, is usually a very slow process for many species. For example, with tulips it takes 5-7 years before the first flower is observed by the breeder. Thus, it is almost exclusively used for the creation of new cultivars, but some bulbs, e.g. Anemone's, are produced commercially by seeds.

PROPAGATION SYSTEMS

There are two types of Natural Propagation Systems for bulbs. These are:

1 - **seed**

2 - **asexual systems.** There are 6 types of natural asexual propagation systems.

a/ annual replacement types

b/ A perennial-type mother bulb with off-set bulblet production

c/ runner-types

d/ stem bulblets

e/ scale bulblets

f/ aerial bulblets (bulbils)

In addition, there are 6 types of Artificial Propagation Systems that have been developed for bulbs. These are:

1 - **Sectioning of selected mother bulbs**

    a/ scaling
    b/ cutting of bulbs

2 - **Scooping or scoring of selected mother bulbs**
3 - **Stem cuttings**
4 - **Leaf cuttings**
5 - **Artificial mutation systems**
6 - **Tissue culture**

These various propagation systems are briefly described in this chapter. It should be pointed out that whenever an asexual system is used it is possible to develop selected clones of a given bulb. Basically, this is what is done when a spontaneous mutant is found within an existing cultivar and then it is separated and developed into a new cultivar. In contrast, there is usually large variability when propagation is carried out by seed. In some instances, however, the varibilities can be rather small and seed systems are used for commercial bulb production (see below).

Natural propagation systems

Seed production The sexual method of producing bulbs by seed is used in 2 ways. First, new cultivars are produced by plant breeders. Second, some bulbs are produced for commercial sale from seed.

Breeding of new cultivars

As far as breeding for new cultivars is concerned, this is a practice conducted by not only scientists at various government laboratories and research stations but also by commercial bulb growers and some very knowledgeable bulb gardeners. There is always the quest for a bulb that has better or more unusual horticultural characteristics. This has been going on for centuries and, since perfection is rarely achieved, will undoubtedly continue forever. Thus, gardeners can always look forward to something new.

The exact techniques used for breeding new cultivars varies with each species. In general, however, controlled crosses are made. Subsequently, the seed are collected, stored, germinated and the seedlings grown until the flower and plant characteristics are effectively evaluated. In addition, bulb resistance to various diseases and its ability to reproduce must be evaluated. Thus, the entire progress takes many years and many resources before the breeder can release a new cultivar. In addition, it explains why new cultivars are more costly than established ones.

BULBS FROM SEEDS - There are several bulbs that are commercially produced by seed. Depending on the species, it can take from 1 to 3 years to produce commercial sized bulbs. Examples of bulbs that are commercially produced from seed are: RANUNCULUS, some ANEMONE'S, some TUBEROUS BEGONIAS, some ALLIUM'S, CHIONODOXA, ERANTHIS, FRITILLARIA MELEAGRIS, AND PUSHKINIA LIBANOTICA.

Annual replacement
In this system, the mother bulb flowers only once in its lifetime and then it is replaced by one or more daughter bulbs. Thus, these bulbs are really annuals.

The TULIP is an example of this type of system (see photograph above). In this instance, a single mother was planted and four daughter bulbs were harvested, 1 large, 1 medium and 2 small sized bulbs. This is what is strived for in commercial bulb production and in perennialization of tulips in the garden.

The GLADIOLUS is an example of corms that reproduce in this manner (see photograph below). In this case, a few large corms were formed from the mother corms and also several cormlets. These can be replanted and increased in size.

Examples of 'Bulbs' with a replacement type propagation system are: ALLIUM'S, BRODIAEA, CAMASSIA, CROCUS, EREMURUS, ERYTHRONIUM, FRITILLARIA IMPERIALIS, GALANTHUS, IRIS, IXIA, IXIOLIRION, ORNITHOGALUM, SCILLA'S AND SPARAXIS.

Newly harvested gladiolus corms: clearly visible are the old, shrivelled mother corm, the new primary corm, and the clusters of cormlets.

Perennial-type mother bulb with offset bulblet production

In this system, the mother bulb persists for several years and as the bulb grows it produces offset bulblets at the side of the mother bulb. Some of the most persistant bulbs in the garden are in this category. They include: some ANEMONE'S, ERANTHIS, HYACINTH'S, MUSCARI'S, NARCISSUS, and AMARYLLIS.

Runner-type

Bulbs in this category form either stolons, rhizomes or droppers. Examples of bulbs with these systems include: CONVALLARIA, RHIZOMTOUS IRIS, GERANIUM TUBEROSUM, TRITELEIA UNIFLORA and SPECIES TULIPS that form the droppers.

Stem bulblets

In this system, axillary buds are formed at the nodes of underground portions of the stems. These underground buds are called 'stem bulblets'. Some lilies are propagated by this system.

Scale bulblets

Lilies are the best example of this system. In this instance, scales are sloughed off and a new bulblet is formed on the scale. It is the basis of the artificial scaling system that will be subsequently described.

Aerial bulblets (Bulbils)

Another system in which axillary buds are used for propagation is with aerial bulblets that are called bulbils. In this case, bulblets are formed either in the leaf axils or in some instances in the floral parts. Examples of this system are: LILIES, TULIPS (Mostly Botanical Species), and BEGONIA EVENSIANA.

Artificial propagation systems
Sectioning of selected mother bulbs

Scaling

This is a system used for propagating lilies. It is illustrated on page 155. Mother bulbs that are free from serious diseases are selected, the scales are carefully removed, dipped in fungicides, and then placed in a sterilized medium. Subsequently, they are maintained in controlled temperature conditions with a high humidity. New bulblets form adventitously on the interior basal part of the scale. This bulblet then forms roots and leaves. The bulblets can be planted out either early in the fall or spring depending on when the bulbs were scaled.

Cutting of bulbs

This is a technique in which selected mother bulbs are carefully cut into segments that will develop new bulblets. Normally, this procedure is used for bulbs like AMARYLLIS (see photograph on right), NARCISSUS, ALLIUM'S, and FRITILLARIA IMPERIALIS. It can also be done with DAHLIAS and TUBEROUS BEGONIAS, but with these species very few bulbs are obtained.

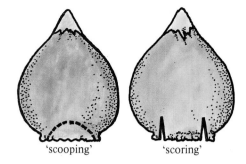

'scooping'   'scoring'

When the bulbs are cut, a clean sharp knife must be used. With the true bulbs, a piece of the basal plate is normally kept with the scales. The pieces are dipped in fungicides and placed in a sterilized planting medium. They are then held under controlled temperature and humidity conditions until the bulblets are formed and ready for transplanting.

Scooping or scoring of selected mother bulbs
For Hyacinths, 2 artificial systems have been developed (see photographs on left). In one case, the basal plate is carefully scooped out. This gives rise to many bulblets and normally takes 3 years to produce commercial sized bulbs. In the other case, the basal plate is scored (cut). This gives rise to fewer, but larger bulblets. As a result, commercial sized bulbs are produced in 2 years. As with the scaling and cutting system, the bulbs must be stored under controlled temperature and humidity conditions until the bulblets are formed. The mother bulbs are planted out in the fall and the bulblets separated the following summer. They are then grown as single bulbs until they reach a commercial flowering size.

Section of an Anemone tuber; it normally, however, reproduces by seed.

A scooped (above) and a scored (below) hyacinth bulb: the clusters of bulblets are clearly visible.

Section of an Amaryllis bulb.
The new bulblets are formed on the scales of the mother bulb.

Stem cuttings

This system is used for DAHLIAS. Selected tuberous-roots are planted in a greenhouse in late winter. When shoots develop from the crowns, stem cuttings are removed being certain that a piece of the crown is taken with the cutting. The cuttings are rooted and the young plants transplanted to the field after the danger of frost has past.

Leaf cuttings

In the system, portions of leaves are cut and then rooted to produce new plants. HAEMANTHUS can propagated by this system.

Artificial mutation systems

In addition to spontaneous mutations that give rise to new cultivars, mutations can be induced by use of various radiation techniques. This is, of course, a specialized system and requires scientific equipment that is not available to the gardener. Mutation breeding has been carried out on a number of bulbs including TULIPS, HYACINTHS, DUTCH IRIS, and DAHLIAS.

2. They are planted in a container and covered with clear plastic wrap.

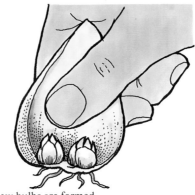

3. The new bulbs are formed in about 6-7 weeks.

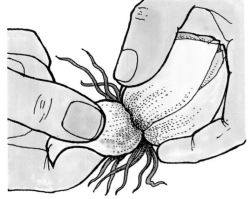

1. The scales are carefully removed from the lily bulb.

4. These are planted and left to grow into fully developed bulbs.

Tissue culture

Again, this is a very specialized system of plant propagation. It requires sterile equipment and facilities and specific media to develop the bulblets in an IN VITRO situation. New bulblets have been developed from scales, leaf sections, axillary buds, scapes, and floral tissue. Investigations have been carried out with many bulb species. Commercially, however, it is most widely used with lilies not only to obtain virus-free clones but also to rapidly increase new cultivars. We will continue to see increased commercial use of tissue culture propagation as the techniques become easier to use and better understood.

Pod with tulip seed.

Daffodil field in flower.

Diseases and insects of bulbs

In general, there are only a few serious diseases and insects that affect bulbs in the garden. In addition, if healthy high quality bulbs were purchased or those bulbs that are already in the garden have been properly cared for, success is relatively easy to achieve and most serious problems can be avoided.

It should be pointed out that the bulb growers and exporters take every precaution possible to deliver bulbs free from serious diseases or pests. Moreover, the bulbs are frequently checked by qualified plant pathologists.

However, as with all other plants, there is no total escape from pests. Although it is rather easy to control insects and other pests as soon as they appear, it is almost impossible to do so against diseases that carry over from the previous growing season. In these instances, complete destruction of the plants is the only remedy. Therefore, maximum precautions must be taken before planting the bulbs. Also during the growth period, bulbs must be observed for the appearance of pests.

A clean, healthy and **WELL-DRAINED SOIL** is the best way to start. If bulbs have been planted for many years in the same area, a soil fumigation may be needed. Also, it is important to kill insects such as aphids which transmit diseases, especially viruses.

We do not cite the names of the fungicides and insecticides that are available. A great number of them are for sale. For specific assistance, contact your local extension office. In addition, some of them are poisonous and we urge gardeners to carefully read the instructions on the packages and to use the pesticides accordingly.

FUSARIUM
Plants grow very slow, then turn yellow and die. If the plant is dug up, you will notice that the bulb is mummied and covered with reddish patches.
Remedies: Plant only healthy bulbs. If bulbs become diseased, they must be removed and destroyed. If bulbs are to be planted in a bed that has BOTRYTIS, it must be fumigated.
Principal species attacked: CYCLAMEN, LILY, NARCISSUS, TULIPS.

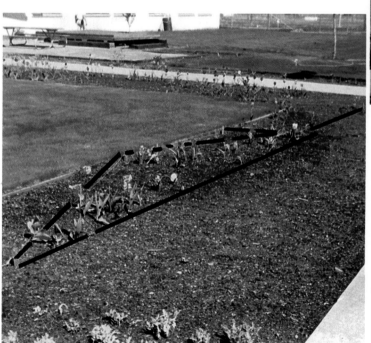

BULBS FAIL TO COME UP

There are four major reasons why such failures can occur:
a/ Bulbs were planted late in the fall, shortly before severe cold weather set in. Therefore, they did not get a chance to develop adequate roots and the freezing temperatures killed them.
Had the beds been covered with a mulch or a good snowcover before severe winter set in, they could probably have survived.
b/ Bulbs were planted in the fall in very dry soil. Due to lack of moisture, they failed to develop adequate roots and freezing weather killed them. (Bulbs will probably be "mushy" when dug up)
c/ Soil p^H was below 5.5 or above 7.3. This can also produce failure.
d/ Poor drainage can also cause serious problems (see illustrations).

The principal diseases

MOSAIC DISEASE (Viruses)

This disease is especially noticable on tulips. If the plants flower they show the beautifully broken effects that is characteristic of the famous Rembrandt tulips. Nowadays, these cultivars are healthy and have a constant spotted and striped color design. Yellow patches and stripes can also appear on the foliage. With the exception of the Rembrandt cultivars, the disease can be spread from plant to plant by aphids.

Remedies: Plants showing the symptoms should be removed.

Principal species attacked: TULIPS, LILIES.

BOTRYTIS SPP.

A disease characterized by small reddish-brown spots. Initially, they usually appear on the leaves, then on the stems and flowers. If allowed to develop a greyish web, it may kill the whole plant. If the diseases attacks the flowers, there is usually a poor floral show.

Remedies: Plant only healthy bulbs. If bulbs become diseased, they must be removed and destroyed. If bulbs are to be planted in a bed that has BOTRYTIS, it must be fumigated.

Principal species attacked: CYCLAMEN, HYACINTHS, NARCISSUS, TULIPS.

RHIZOCTONIA (Bulb rot)

Various forms of this disease occur especially with Tulips and Hyacinths and the symptoms differ accordingly. There can be poor growth of shoots and a total rotting of the bulbs.

Remedies: Plant only healthy bulbs. If bulbs become diseased, they must be removed and destroyed. If bulbs are to be planted in a bed that has RHIZOCTONIA, it must be fumigated.

BOTRYTIS ELLIPTICA

A disease that especially attacks lilies and GLADIOLUS during humid periods. It is characterized by reddish-brown spots on the leaves.

Remedies: Fumigate the soil before planting and spray with an approved fungicide. Heavily infected plants must be removed. Lilies left in the ground should be sprayed with a fungicide three to four times a year.

Principal pests

MITES AND THRIPS

Bulb mites - Hyacinths and Narcissus
Wheat curl mite - Tulips
Gladiolus thrips - Gladiolus, Iris, Lilies.

Mites are minute and sometimes microscopic acarines, while thrips are larger. They can form large colonies on the plants, suck up the sap and cause patches and stripes in different colors. The bulbs may also be attacked.

Remedies: Spray with approved insecticides or miticides. Destroy any heavily infected bulbs.

SLUGS

Slug can eat the roots and softer parts of the bulbs in the night and leave behind slimy traces.

Remedies: The best results are obtained by using slug baits placed beneath the mulch or on small boards or flats. The slugs can also be physically removed and destroyed.

APHIDS

Carriers of numerous diseases, and especially viruses, aphids are one of the most serious pests for all plants. They form large colonies and can cover leaves, stems, and flowers. They produce a honey-like substance that draws ants, flies and other insects. Generally they occur near the end of spring, when temperatures begin to rise.

Remedies: Spray the plants with an approved insecticide as soon as aphids are observed.

OTHER PESTS

Mice and some other rodents are fond of bulbs, especially TULIPS and CROCUS. For a small planting, the bulbs can be covered with special frames that have a wire-netting. That has holes large enough to let the shoots growth through, but too small for the animals to penetrate.

Close-up of a Tulip flower
showing the pistil and 6 anthers.

INDEX